Primary School Kit
on the
United Nations

Editors
David Barrs
Maura Juffkins

Illustrators
Julie Beer
Jason Newman
Tracy Smith

Cover illustration
From *Motherhood* – a painting by Ting Shao Kuang

This project was made possible with support from Felissimo, Fundacion Amalia Lacroze de Fortabat and Goldstar.

Global sponsors of the United Nations Fiftieth Anniversary Commemoration and the Foundation for the Fiftieth Anniversary of the United Nations, Inc.

For information and orders contact:

UN Publications
Sales Office and Bookshop
CH–1211
Geneva 10
Switzerland
41-22-917-2614

UN Publications
2 United Nations Plaza
Room DC2–853
Department 007C
New York, NY 10017
212-963-8302

Tables, figures and statistics reproduced in this book are examples chosen for illustrative and pedagogical purposes only.

ISBN 1 85749 205 6
Published by Pearson Publishing Ltd for and on behalf of UN50
© Pearson Publishing Ltd, 1995
Text © UNA-UK, 1995

The *Kits on the United Nations* are based on materials originally provided by UNA-UK.

Contents

Foreword

Boutros Boutros-Ghali
Secretary-General of the United Nations

The international community in the last decade has recognized a new array of global problems – such as environmental degradation, drug trafficking, terrorism and the spread of the AIDS/HIV virus. More recently has come an awareness that age-old problems once considered national matters – such as poverty, joblessness and social breakdown – are now of global scale and concern. In parallel to these challenges, the perennial problem of international peace and security has emerged in new forms that test our collective ability to respond effectively.

In this setting the United Nations is being called into action by its Member States more often and more extensively than ever before. Consequently, knowledge about the United Nations is evermore important for citizens in all walks of life, young and old. It is they who will ensure that their governments recognize the indispensable role of the United Nations in today's world. With their understanding and support, the United Nations can strengthen its work to maintain peace and security, promote social and economic progress and achieve human betterment for all peoples.

The *Primary School Kit on the United Nations* is a contribution to this effort for awareness and education. To all the teachers using the enclosed materials, I send my warm greetings and best wishes for success in this important work. You are an essential component of a worldwide network of committed people who can make a difference for the future of all humankind.

Boutros Boutros-Ghali
Secretary-General

Acknowledgements

This project is a collective achievement and we are indebted to a wide range of teachers who came together in a common purpose – to extend the original **United Nations Kit** into a three tier international project.

Other organizations directly involved with the production of the materials were the Council for Education in World Citizenship, the National Association for Able Children in Education, the British Sports Association for the Disabled, Peace Child International and St Mary's C of E School, Saffron Walden, Essex, UK (who hosted a conference for contributors).

Permissions

We thank the United Nations Photo Unit for permission to reproduce photographs of the following (listed as item, donor and where located at UN headquarters in New York):

- Tapestry of Pablo Picasso's painting *Femme sur l'echelle* (*Woman on a ladder*), Mrs Albert D Lasker (United States); Delegates' south lounge, Conference Building. (Used on the cover of the **Intermediate School Kit on the United Nations**.)
- Bronze sculpture *Let Us Beat Swords into Plowshares* by Evgeny Vuchetich; USSR; North Garden.
- Wool tapestry after Pablo Picasso's *La Guernica* (on loan); Mrs Nelson A Rockefeller; Curved wall on second floor outside Security Council Chamber.
- Marc Chagall's stained glass panel in memory of Dag Hammarskjöld and those who died with him in 1961; United Nations staff and Marc Chagall; Outside Meditation Room, General Assembly public lobby. (Used on the cover of the **Secondary School Kit on the United Nations**.)

We would like to thank the United Nations for permission to reproduce Casal's *United Nations Hymn* and the letter from Jelena Urošević to the Secretary-General and for supplying a variety of statistical and textual data. Thanks also to the World Federation of United Nations Associations and the artist, Ting Shao Kuang, for permission to reproduce *Motherhood* on the cover of the **Primary School Kit on the United Nations**; and to UNICEF for permission to reproduce the Christmas card designed by Jitka Samkova.

We are also grateful to Ponce/El Pais for the "disasters panorama"; Greenpeace Ltd for the use of their passage entitled *The history of the Earth*; G Thomas for R S Thomas' poem entitled *The Evacuee*; and Kathleen Weaver for her translation from French of the poem *All that you have given me, Africa* by Anoma Kanié.

The following copyright sources are most gratefully acknowledged:

- The poems entitled *My only cry: "close the arms factories"* by Leila Ibrahim Semaan and *How many children have died* by Noura Bahi are copyright © UNESCO 1981. Reproduced by permission of UNESCO.

- The extracts from Benjamin Britten's *Voices for Today* come from a number of writers; three lines from *Lies* by Yevgeny Yevtushenko from *Yevtushenko Selected Poems*, translated by Robin Milner-Gulland and Peter Levi, (Penguin Books, 1962), copyright © Robin Milner-Gulland and Peter Levi, 1962; two lines from *Resistance, Rebellion and Death* by Albert Camus, translated by Justin O'Brien, published by Hamish Hamilton and reproduced by permission of Alfred A Knopf Inc. The music extracts from *Voices for Today* are copyright © Faber Music Ltd. Reprinted by permission.

- The poem *Today* by Denise Levertov, from a long poem entitled *Staying Alive* is taken from *Denise Levertov: Poems 1960-1967*, copyright © 1966 by Denise Levertov and used by permission of New Directions Publishing Corporation.

Teacher's Notes

Educating succeeding generations

As international institutions become more important to the day-to-day lives of the world's inhabitants, it becomes ever more imperative that succeeding generations come to understand their function, their limitations and, most of all, their potential.

Key issues facing this and future generations are not confined within national or even regional boundaries. Pollution, migration, conflict, drug trafficking, disease and unemployment are global issues. In educating the global citizen, the purpose is to illuminate how personal, national and global interests are linked. We live in one world – we breathe the same air, use the same water, depend on the same resources and share the same emotions. In a very real sense, global issues are relevant to preparing young people for life in an increasingly interdependent world. The global village becomes more and more real for each succeeding generation. There is also a legal case for incorporating an international dimension to our teaching. As Member States of the United Nations, Articles 55 and 56 of the Charter call on us to promote 'educational cooperation'.

As with any other educational activity, teaching about global issues carries an additional responsibility: to allow people to express their hopes for the world's future and enable them to act on those. If such opportunities are not offered to students, educators run the risk of creating generations of cynics and unaware, narrow-minded citizens – people both indifferent to the issues and powerless to act. The materials in the **Kits on the United Nations** are designed to provide knowledge and understanding but also to empower students. The materials are based on two assumptions. Firstly, that education matters and can make a difference to the quality of life of individuals. Secondly, that the cooperation of Member States within the structure of the UN is in our common interest and has the potential to make increasingly positive contributions in an interdependent world.

These materials introduce students to the UN and many of the global issues and concerns it addresses – although the scope of the work of the UN system is so wide-ranging that not all of it can be covered within the confines of a kit such as this. Relevant information on the UN and its work is included in each unit, but these can only be examined, taught and understood within the context of the larger issues and ideals. As an organization of Member States, a community of nations, the UN is dedicated to the pursuit of peace, justice and development on behalf of people everywhere. It is important to realise, however, that the UN is not a government in itself. Its effectiveness depends on the collective will of the Member States and citizens within those countries.

The constitution of UNESCO states that "...war begins in the minds of men and it is in the minds of men that the forces of peace must be constructed...". UNESCO is 50 years old in 1996 and that statement is as relevant today as it was in 1946. These materials have been motivated by that ideal. Succeeding generations of young people must be introduced to the work of the UN, its Funds, Programmes and Agencies.

Objectives

While acquisition of factual knowledge has always been a specific educational goal, this curriculum places equal emphasis on thinking about perceptions and behaviours. International education should be directed towards the promotion of human survival – a joint effort to battle inequality, injustice and the use of force. To this end, the activities have been designed not only to sharpen the student's comprehension skills, but also to engage students in reflecting on their environment as well as on their behaviour; to examine the interdependent world in which they live and understand their ability to shape that world.

Teachers should be aware of the strong emphasis on group activities. As in the work and goals of the UN, so here cooperation and consensus-building play a crucial role. The purpose of collaborative work and debate is to promote respect for different perspectives, encourage discussion as a way of finding solutions to common problems, and generate critical and open thinking about each subject. The principles of the UNESCO Special Needs Project* have influenced the design of the activities.

Equally important are participation and empowerment. Students should realise that they can be active in the local and international communities. Several activities ask students to find out about local and international organizations working in their area. They should be aware that as young people they can often join or work with such organizations. The objective is not to provide easy answers, nor to suggest that the UN has been a panacea for global problems. Students should be encouraged to debate and discuss the issues as well as the UN's role in dealing with the issues. To this end, activities in each unit have been designed so that they can be used as the basis for a detailed research project or for short classroom discussions.

Using the kits

The project is available at three levels: the **Primary School Kit on the United Nations** (7-11 year olds), **Intermediate School Kit on the United Nations** (11-14 year olds), **Secondary School Kit on the United Nations** (14-16 year olds). The ages are offered for general guidance only. The kits can be used within the context of a broader school or national curriculum or as a self-contained package.

All three kits are organized along a similar line, using the ideals of the UN as guiding concepts. Conflict prevention, human rights and sustainable development – three fields in which the UN is active – are the organizing categories of the kits.

The kits are arranged in sequence. First, they introduce the UN, its history and basic principles; then they delve into the UN's work in the following order: conflict prevention and resolution, human rights and sustainable development. Five *Backgrounders* at the beginning of the kits introduce the UN to the teacher. *Resource Points* at the end of the kits are there to provide the teacher with additional reference and support material. These concerns, rather than a given subject such as Geography or Mathematics, have determined the sequence of the units. Hence units on specific subject matters may be interspersed in the kits. But as subject matters are indicated at the top of the units, teachers who opt to teach only those units that fit within their subject areas may easily do so. Such an approach, however, would be enhanced if it were to be carried out in conjunction with other teachers – for instance, a geography, a history and a science teacher.

Each unit is split into a main text, a *UN Factfile* and activities. While the main text presents the subject and the theme, the activities are the focal points of the units. They encourage critical and creative thinking, participation, and reflection on one's own attitudes and behaviour. The *UN Factfiles* are meant to present the student with specific examples of UN involvement. They should be used as sources of information, but they also demonstrate how an international organization can improve life for citizens of all countries.

* UNESCO Special Needs Project, Special Educations Programme, UNESCO, F-75352 Paris 07SP, France

At least one of the activities will require the student to have read and understood the *Factfile*. The symbol of the swallow, a bird flying high and seeking out new possibilities, has been used to indicate extension activities.

Suggestions for additional activities

The following activities are suggestions for year-round projects that should not require additional text books or staff. Some of these activities may also appear in the kits, but they are included here because they are flexible enough to enrich students of all age levels.

1 United Nations Week: While individual teachers will see opportunities for using individual sheets in their lessons, the most successful use of the materials is likely to be cross-curricular. A United Nations Week, close to 24 October, which is United Nations Day, could involve teachers of all subjects working together. Schools worldwide are encouraged to take part in a "Global Teach-In", that is, to dedicate a day or even a week to the study of the United Nations and issues on its global agenda. The week might culminate in a whole school or whole year group event such as an inter-class quiz, a Model United Nations or a conference on a global issue. Each subject department could agree to use some or all of the units relevant to their subject. The advantage of this approach in terms of cross-curricular work is that all teachers can contribute on the basis of their subject strength rather than be asked to temporarily abandon their subject expertise in the interests of a cross-curricular theme. If subject teachers can cooperate in this way, the educational experience for the students will be, rather like the United Nations itself, greater than the sum of the parts.

2 A Class Charter: Ask the class to draw up a Class Charter. This could be based on the Preamble to the UN Charter (*Resource Point E*) or it could simply be rules developed by the students themselves; the purpose, however, should be the same: to avoid conflict and make sure everyone is treated fairly and equally. Without enforcing the Class Charter, see if its rules work as the year progresses. Do they need to be added to? Changed? If so the majority of the class must agree to the changes. Students need to persuade others that the proposed changes are needed. The other part of a Charter is its enforcement. Are its rules and principles obeyed? If not, how could they be enforced with fairness and respect for the equality of all students?

3 A United School: The school, or at least a number of grades within the school, can be turned into a mini-UN to address school-wide concerns and issues. There are many ways to do this and the following basic suggestions are taken from the Northeast International School in New Jersey, US, which has a UN system for grades 2-5. Each class can be a country with a fictitious name and vote for two representatives. The representatives of each class will go to a general assembly which will have to agree on a charter and sign it. If there are any concerns – unequal treatment, noise, classes interfering in the conduct of other classes, etc – these can be taken to the general assembly which can then decide what to do. The assembly can also create councils to take care of the school garden, news, sports or any other programmes.

4 A Global Citizen Newsletter: The class can put together a newsletter about world concerns and their effects on students' own communities. This would, ideally, identify and emphasise global interdependency. Students can write to UN Information Centres or UN Associations for additional information (see *Resource Point K*), use news clippings, radio and TV reports, or go out and find stories in their own communities. If needed, the class can be split into groups responsible for specific tasks (eg newsletter layout, reporting, production, etc) or issues (eg an environmental group, a peace and security group, an arts group, etc).

The International Baccalaureate Organisation (IBO)

The International Baccalaureate Organisation promotes academic achievement coupled with active and responsible world citizenship. The IB Diploma programme (ages 16-19) is a pre-university curriculum offered by more than 550 authorised member schools in 75 countries. The Middle Years Programme, designed for the 11-16 age range, similarly emphasises the dynamic combination of knowledge, experience and critical thinking. Headquartered in Geneva* with principal offices in Cardiff, New York, Buenos Aires and Singapore, the IBO enjoys cordial relationships with governments, ministries of education, universities and many United Nations agencies.

The *Intermediate* and *Secondary School Kits on the United Nations* are organised according to the curriculum model of the International Baccalaureate Organisation's Middle Years Programme. The *Primary School Kit on the United Nations* is organized according to the key concerns of the project (Sustainable Development, Human Rights and Conflict Prevention and Resolution) since a strict subject classification was considered inappropriate at this level.

Symbol used in the Kits	Subjects	Suggested United Nations teaching contexts
Book	Language A	Debate on UN Reform, Human Rights UN Charter, Peacekeeping, ILO, UNHCR, W H Auden
World	History	UN Charter, League of Nations, Decolonisation, Conflict, Declaration of Human Rights, UNESCO
	Geography	FAO, UNEP, WMO, UNFPA, UNHCR, HABITAT, UNDP
Person	Humanities	ILO, UN Special Committee Against Apartheid, UNESCO
Microscope	Sciences Biology Physics Chemistry	Oral Health, Microbiology, Earth Summit Atomic Energy Energy
Calculator	Mathematics	UN Budget, UN Member States
Cogs	Technology	UNDP, UNEP, FAO, IAEA, WHO
Masks	Arts Art Music Drama	Marc Chagall, Pablo Picasso, UN logos Pablo Casals, Anthems Health Education, UNESCO
Ball and racket	Physical Education	WHO, Human Rights

Note: The IB also incorporates a Language B (Foreign Language) which, for the purposes of this project, has not been included.

* For more information contact: Communications Department, International Baccalaureate Organisation, 15 Route des Morillons, 1218 Grand-Saconnex, Geneva, Switzerland.

The Middle Years Programme is given coherence through Areas of Interaction which are addressed both within and across the programme:

- Approaches to Learning – learning how to learn
- Community Service – first hand experience in the local setting and wider world
- Health and Social Education – preparing for a physically and mentally healthy life
- Environment – explains conservation and stewardship
- *Homo faber* ('Man the Maker') – appreciate the human capacity to transform, enjoy and improve quality of life over time.

Students are required to complete a Personal Project based on their experience of the Areas of Interaction.

Within the IBMYP the 'Areas of Interaction' give the programme a vital coherence. They permeate the materials and provide interesting opportunities for colleagues in different curriculum areas to work collaboratively (see diagram below).

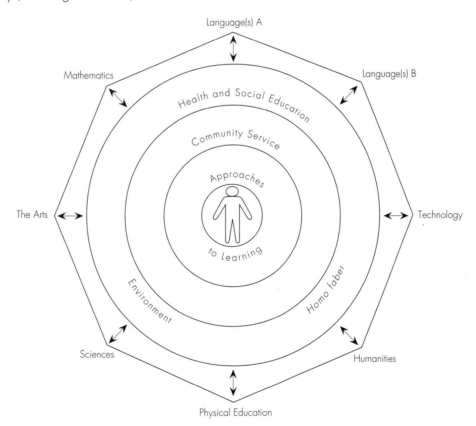

A note on style

Preparing a manuscript which deals with a broad-ranging international organization such as the United Nations inevitably raises questions of style. When appropriate the official UN Standard has been used. For instance, the term Member State is shown with capital letters throughout. All but one of the UN Agencies with the 'Organization' in their title spell it with a 'z'. The exception is the International Labour Organisation.

In view of the likely confusion that this will create for children, it is worth explaining it from the outset.

The United Nations and its Charter

The United Nations

The United Nations officially came into existence on 24 October 1945, when the UN Charter had been ratified by a majority of the original 51 Member States. The day is now celebrated each year around the world as United Nations Day.

The purpose of the United Nations is to bring all nations of the world together to work for peace and development, based on the principles of justice, human dignity and the well-being of all people. It affords the opportunity for countries to balance global interdependence and national interests when addressing international problems.

There are currently (March 1995) 185 Members of the United Nations. They meet in the General Assembly, which is the closest thing to a world parliament. Each country, large or small, rich or poor, has a single vote, however, none of the decisions taken by the Assembly are binding. Nevertheless, the Assembly's decisions become resolutions that carry the weight of world governmental opinion.

The United Nations Headquarters is in New York City but the land and buildings are international territory. The United Nations has its own flag, its own post office and its own postage stamps. Six official languages are used at the United Nations – Arabic, Chinese, English, French, Russian and Spanish. The UN European Headquarters is in the Palais des Nations, Geneva, Switzerland. It has an office in Vienna, Austria and Economic Commissions in Addis Ababa in Ethiopia, Amman in Jordan, Bangkok in Thailand and Santiago in Chile. The senior officer of the United Nations Secretariat is the Secretary-General.

The UN logo shows the world held in the 'olive branches of peace'

The predecessor

The League of Nations was founded immediately after the First World War. It originally consisted of 42 countries, 26 of which were non-European. At its largest, 57 countries were members of the League. The League was created because a number of people in France, South Africa, the UK and the US believed that a world organization of nations could keep the peace and prevent a repetition of the horrors of the 1914-18 war in Europe. An effective world body now seemed possible because communications were so much better and there was increasing experience of working together in international organizations. Coordination and cooperation for economic and social progress were becoming important.

The League had two basic aims. Firstly, it sought to preserve the peace through collective action. Disputes would be referred to the League's Council for arbitration and conciliation. If necessary, economic and then military sanctions could be used. In other words, members undertook to defend other members from aggression. Secondly, the League aimed to promote international cooperation in economic and social affairs.

The Covenant of the League of Nations begins...

"In order to promote international cooperation and to achieve international peace and security by the acceptance of obligations not to resort to war, by the prescription of open, just and honourable relations between nations, by the firm establishment of the understandings of international law as the actual rule of conduct among Governments, and by the maintenance of justice and a scrupulous respect for all treaty obligations in the dealings of organised peoples with one another, Agree to this Covenant of the League of Nations."

The end of the League

As the Second World War unfolded, it became clear that the League had failed in its chief aim of keeping the peace. The League had no military power of its own. It depended on its members' contributions; and its members were not willing to use sanctions, economic or military. Moral authority was insufficient.

Several Big Powers failed to support the League: the United States crucially never joined; Germany was a member for only seven years from 1926 and the USSR for only five years from 1934; Japan and Italy both withdrew in the 30s. The League then depended mainly on Britain and France, who were understandably hesitant to act forcefully. It was indeed difficult for governments long accustomed to operating independently to work through this new organization.

The UN Charter

Even as the Second World War raged, the leaders of Britain, China, the US and the USSR, under intense pressure from the press and public, discussed the details of a post-war organization. In 1944 representatives of China, the UK, the US and the USSR meeting at Dumbarton Oaks in Washington, DC, prepared a blueprint for an international organization. Towards the end of the war representatives of 50 countries gathered in San Francisco between April and June 1945 to hammer out the final text that would lay the foundations of international cooperation. This was the Charter of the United Nations, signed on 26 June by 50 countries. Poland, the 51st country, was not able to send a representative to the conference but is considered an original member. Although the League was abandoned, most of its ideals and some of its structure were kept by the United Nations and outlined in its Charter. The ideals of peace and social and economic progress remained the basic goals of the new world organization. However, these were developed to fit the new and more complex post-war world.

The League's Council was transformed into the Security Council consisting of the five victors of the war as permanent members and ten other countries serving two year terms. The five permanent members – China, France, the UK, the USSR, and the US were also given veto power, which means that decisions taken by the Security Council can be blocked by any of the five permanent members. This is significant firstly because the Security Council is the principle UN organ responsible for ensuring peace, and, secondly, because it is the only body whose decisions are binding on all Member States. Since the creation of the UN the balance of Big Powers has changed and over one hundred new Member States, mainly non-Western, have joined. With these changes have come increasing demands to reform the Security Council.

The brief provision for 'Social Activities' in the League's Covenant was turned into a comprehensive prescription for international economic and social cooperation, with the aim of achieving conditions of stability and well-being recognised as essential for peaceful relations among nations. Under the aegis of a new organ, the Economic and Social Council, the work of existing and anticipated Specialized Agencies in the fields of labour, education, health, agriculture, development and many others would be coordinated within the UN system. Racism and repression demanded that another, new, people's element should enter emphatically into the Charter, that of rights. Many sorts of rights, from the right to self-determination, which encouraged the independence of colonized peoples, to general human rights, which aimed to protect individuals, are enshrined in the Charter, the Universal Declaration of Human Rights and two Covenants which have become major, standard-setting additions to international law.

The UN System

The basic structure of the United Nations is outlined in *Resource Point C*. What the structure does not show is that decision-making within the UN system is not as easy as in many other organizations. The UN is not an independent, homogeneous organization; it is made up of states, so actions by the UN depend on the will of Member States, to accept, fund or carry them out. Especially in matters of peace-keeping and international politics, it requires a complex, often slow, process of consensus-building that must take into account national sovereignty as well as global needs.

The Specialized Agencies, while part of the UN system, are separate, autonomous intergovernmental organizations which work with the UN and with each other. The agencies carry out work relating to specific fields such as trade, communications, air and maritime transport, agriculture and development. Although they have more autonomy, their work within a country or between countries is always carried out in partnership with those countries. They also depend on funds from Member States to achieve their goals.

Recently, international conferences organised by the UN have gained significance. UN conferences have been held since the 60s, but with the Conference on Environment and Development, known as the Earth Summit, in Rio de Janeiro, Brazil, in 1992, they turned into real forums for deciding on national and international policy regarding issues that affect everyone such as the environment, human rights and economic development. Since the Rio conference, UN conferences have turned into forums in which non-governmental organizations (NGOs) can voice their concerns alongside those of governments. Such conferences focus world attention on these issues and place them squarely on the global agenda, but once the international agreements produced by these conferences are signed, it is still up to each individual country to carry them out. Yet, with the moral weight of international conferences and the pressures of media and NGOs, Member States are more likely to endorse the agreements and put them into effect.

The aims of the United Nations:

- To keep peace throughout the world.
- To develop friendly relations between nations.
- To work together to help people live better lives, to eliminate poverty, disease and illiteracy in the world, to stop environmental destruction and to encourage respect for each other's rights and freedoms.
- To be a centre for helping nations achieve these aims.

The principles of the United Nations:

- All Member States have sovereign equality.
- All Member States must obey the Charter.
- Countries must try to settle their differences by peaceful means.
- Countries must avoid using force or threatening to use force.
- The UN may not interfere in the domestic affairs of any country.
- Countries should try to assist the United Nations.

Conflict Prevention and Resolution

"We the peoples of the United Nations (are) determined to save succeeding generations from the scourge of war, which twice in our lifetime has brought untold sorrow to mankind."

Preamble to the United Nations Charter

Preventive diplomacy (or preventing conflict) is action to stop disputes before they flare into military conflicts. This can involve early warning, mediation, fact-finding and confidence building.	**Peace-making** is action to settle conflicts through peaceful means such as negotiations, judicial settlements, sanctions or cease-fire agreements.	**Peace-keeping**, often involves placing persons – civilian and military – between hostile parties to help control and resolve a conflict. Peace-keepers wear blue helmets or blue berets. In 1988, the UN peace-keepers were awarded the Nobel Peace Prize.	**Peace-building** (or building the peace) involves attempts at reconstruction (or re-building) and reconciliation (or to re-establish friendly relations). Through establishing projects which link hostile parties together, the hope is to create confidence which is necessary for peace.

The UN has various means it can use to help resolve conflicts:

 Member States may bring a conflict to the attention of the Security Council. The Security Council can then call upon countries in conflict to settle their differences peacefully (Article 33).

 If countries in conflict can't come to an agreement on their own, they can take the dispute to the International Court of Justice which will decide who is right and who is wrong (Article 36).

 The Security Council may ask United Nations members to stop trading with the country or countries and to cut all forms of communication including by sea, air, rail, post, telephone, radio etc. Members may also be asked to close Embassies in the country or countries concerned (Article 41).

 If all this fails, or is felt to be impractical, the Security Council may dispatch neutral UN peace-keepers to patrol safety or demilitarised zones, or to enforce or monitor cease-fire agreements, until a permanent agreement is reached. However, peacekeepers can only be sent if all countries in conflict agree to their presence.

 In some cases, the Security Council may authorise Member States to intervene in a conflict by using a regular military force. Forces are contributed by Member States, but are not under UN command – this has only happened twice, in Korea in 1950 and in Kuwait in 1991.

 Article 43 requires all Member States to make an agreed number of armed forces available to the Security Council for use in such cases.

These measures can be very effective when you think that the United Nations represents almost the whole world – 185 States (March 1995) altogether. Countries at war would have to think very hard before ignoring world opinion.

Peace-keeping was pioneered by the UN, but it evolved slowly from its first use in 1948. In recent years, however, peace-keeping has gained more importance in situations where preventive diplomacy or peace-making fail. In 1994 there were 17 active peace-keeping operations. There are some important differences between UN peace-keeping forces and other armed forces:
- UN peace-keepers cannot take sides in a conflict
- Countries in conflict must agree to the presence of peace-keepers
- UN peace-keepers are generally lightly armed and cannot use force unless attacked
- UN peace-keepers may also be police and other civilians because peace-keeping includes a range of activities including humanitarian assistance, monitoring elections, and observing and reporting on a situation.

Human Rights

The Universal Declaration of Human Rights 1948

"Fundamental human rights" is the second item in the Preamble to the Charter of the UN, after "the scourge of war". Increasingly it is being recognised that abuse of human rights is the cause of conflicts. As early as 1948 the UN produced the Universal Declaration of Human Rights. These are standards that aim to protect the individual citizen from abuses. The Universal Declaration states that human rights are "the foundation of freedom, justice and peace in the world."

The Universal Declaration is a standard, but it is not law. However, several covenants, which include the main points of the Declaration, were signed in the 1960s and came into force in 1976 after most of the countries had ratified them. That was a turning point because it meant that the countries that had signed and ratified the agreements were obliged to abide by them. They also gave the right to the UN to monitor whether or not governments are observing their citizens' human rights.

Human rights

Not all rights are of the same type. Some are concerned with civil and political freedoms and equality before the law, but others need investment of money from the country concerned for them to be available to its citizens – an example of this is the right to education. But these are still rights, even if they cannot yet be fully implemented.

The Universal Declaration says that all people are born free and equal in dignity and rights, and that they should not be discriminated against because of their nationality, ethnicity, religion, race, gender, political opinion, wealth or property. These are some of the rights spelled out in the Declaration: freedom from slavery; freedom from torture; equal protection of the law, freedom from arbitrary arrest and the right to a fair trial; freedom of thought, opinion, religion and expression; the right to education; the right to an adequate standard of living, including good health, shelter and enough food; the right to work and to form and join trade unions.

Human rights protection depends on good information. People need to know what their rights are and to be able to report when they are infringed. This is largely the work of non-governmental organizations (NGOs), such as Amnesty International, who can tell the UN Human Rights Commission which collects information. Individuals can tell the UN High Commissioner for Human Rights about human rights abuses. Protection also depends on governments and people fulfilling their duty or obligation to respect human rights.

Refugees

Refugees often find themselves in situations where their human rights are infringed. The UN High Commissioner for Refugees (UNHCR) is responsible for protecting refugees, because their own countries will not or can not. Altogether that is about 20 million people worldwide. In addition there are estimated to be 25 million displaced people. Most refugees are hoping they can be repatriated when it is safe to return home.

Most refugees are in the developing world because that is where most conflicts are taking place. At least 80% are women and children. They need emergency help which UNHCR provides, often through NGOs, but they may have to stay in camp for years and will need education and training. Refugees have to be very adaptable in order to survive and are an asset both to the countries they seek asylum in and to their own countries when they are able to return.

Key words

ratify	when a country ratifies a treaty or convention, they agree to abide by what it says
rapporteur	someone who reports on a situation
asylum-seeker	someone who asks another country for permission to stay in safety
displaced	people who have had to leave home
refugee	a person who has left their country due to a well-founded fear of persecution because of their race, religion, nationality, political opinion or social group
repatriated	a refugee who returns home
migrant	someone who has moved to another country looking for a better life or job

Sustainable Development

What is sustainable development?

The UN Environment Programme (UNEP) defines sustainable development as programmes that would "improve people's quality of life within the carrying capacity of the Earth's life-support system." This means meeting the needs of the present generation without damaging the Earth's resources in such a way that would prevent future generations from meeting theirs. Sustainable development also emphasizes equitable development; that is, it regards bridging the gap between rich and poor countries as an important way of ensuring that the generations of today *and* tomorrow can meet their needs.

The UN and sustainable development

Since the United Nations convened the Conference on Human Environment in 1972 in Stockholm, concern has been mounting over the continuous deterioration of the global environment. Should this disruption of the global ecological and economic balances continue, it would jeopardise the Earth's life-sustaining qualities and eventually lead to both ecological and economic catastrophe.

Some of the dangers to the Earth and its population:
- Pollution is damaging the Earth's air and water. Each year, our industries produce millions of tons of hazardous waste which they dump in the seas, landfills, or, worse, in poor countries. These damage the atmosphere, can alter the climate and are poisonous to us as well as to animals.
- Careless use of land is reducing cultivable land. Over-farming and cutting down forests, often in the face of changing climates, lead to soil degradation. As land becomes less and less fertile, those who farm it or use it for its trees lose their source of livelihood.
- Human activity is killing off the variety of life. There are some 30 million species on Earth – this diversity of life around us is called biodiversity. It is from these biological resources that we obtain clothes, medicine, food and housing. The greatest threat to biodiversity comes from the destruction of rainforests. In the Amazon, a single tree can contain 2000 unique species of animals. Rainforests are also essential in maintaining the balance of carbon dioxide in the atmosphere. However, unmanaged logging and agriculture along with acid rain are destroying the rainforests.

Member States of the United Nations stress that economic and environmental degradation are interrelated and that environmental protection in developing countries has to be viewed as an integral part of the development process. At the same time, consumption patterns and production in industrialized countries speed up environmental deterioration. To solve these probems there needs to be new levels of cooperation among nations – a global partnership.

The Earth Summit (1992)

That was the goal of the Earth Summit held in Rio de Janeiro. The United Nations Conference on Environment and Development, or the Earth Summit as it came to be known, was arguably one of the most significant landmarks in the understanding of sustainable development to date.

In Rio, five major agreements were reached by 172 heads of state. Non-governmental organizations (NGOs) were also crucial in helping to frame the agenda. Each agreement deals with specific concerns such as the climate or the forests. One of them, Agenda 21, is an all encompassing plan of action which includes most of the important steps that need to be taken to achieve sustainable development.

These are some of the things Agenda 21 asks governments and their citizens to do:
- recognize the link between environment and development issues
- use energy more efficiently and develop renewable energy sources like wind and solar power
- give farmers environmental education
- plant new forests and replant damaged ones
- eliminate poverty by helping the poor earn a living in a way that doesn't damage the environment
- impose fines on people and industries that pollute the waters
- prepare national plans for waste management
- require that industry adopt safer and cleaner production methods
- change wasteful consumption patterns.

A high level body, the UN Commission on Sustainable Development, was set up to oversee the implementation of all agreements reached in Rio. The UN has also set up offices to help countries reach these goals by helping governments, scientists and local people share information and technology, and by carrying out training programmes so people can learn about sustainable development and how to achieve it.

The United Nations and NGOs

"...Peace in the largest sense cannot be accomplished by the United Nations system or by governments alone. Non-governmental organizations, academic institutions, parliamentarians, business and professional communities, the media and the public at large must all be involved. This will strengthen the world organization's ability to reflect the concerns and interests of its widest constituency..."

An Agenda for Peace, Boutros Boutros-Ghali

What are NGOs?

A non-governmental organization (NGO) is any local, national or international citizens' group (ie, not part of a government) which does not work for profit. This simple definition also means that organizations under the label of NGOs have an extremely broad range of functions. NGOs work in fields as diverse as law, refugee work, human rights and disarmament; their work can range from influencing policy or organizing communities around special issues to providing technical or medical assistance to conducting research.

Over the past decade the role of NGOs in local and international affairs has grown tremendously. By way of example, 54 000 new organizations were set up in France between 1987 and 1994; in less than a decade, 27 000 in Chile. The amount of development assistance flowing through NGOs has more than doubled since 1980. Most of this growth reflects a desire on the part of citizens to influence their own lives and environments. Because of their flexibility, NGOs provide a unique channel through which ordinary citizens can participate in decisions which they feel affect their lives – that could be anything from housing to arms control.

UN and NGOs

In the 1945 San Francisco meetings in which the United Nations Charter was drawn up and signed, 42 NGOs were invited to participate by the US government. They presented draft texts for the Charter, parts of which were eventually incorporated, including this passage from Article 71: *"The Economic and Social Council may make suitable arrangements for consultation with non-governmental organizations..."*. That laid the foundations for cooperation between the UN and NGOs. The Council granted consultative status to a limited number of NGOs, which meant that these NGOs could participate in some debates and, in some cases, place items on the agenda. Other NGOs, however, could cooperate in the field with the specialised agencies.

It was probably in the field more than anywhere else that the presence of NGOs began to be felt strongly. Specialised agencies and bodies such as the UN Development Programme and the UN High Commissioner for Refugees realised early on that NGOs offered them crucial resources and expertise. For example, without the cooperation of humanitarian organisations – ranging from CARE to Médecins Sans Frontières (Doctors Without Borders) – it would have been virtually impossible to meet the needs of refugees fleeing war. Many of these specialised agencies have their own relationships with NGOs; they can coordinate

NGO efforts, provide funds for NGO projects, or even receive funds from NGOs for their own programmes. The cooperation of NGOs has also furthered the goals of the UN in other areas such as disarmament, human rights, education, the environment and science.

Beginning with the 1992 UN Conference on Environment and Development in Rio de Janeiro, the broader participation of NGOs in addressing global issues became a fact. Over 1500 organizations were accredited to participate in the conference. In this and subsequent international conferences, such as the World Conference on Human Rights (Vienna), the International Conference on Population and Development (Cairo), the World Summit for Social Development (Copenhagen) and the Fourth World Conference on Women (Beijing), NGOs have shaped many of the points on the agendas, some of which have already become law.

In short, NGOs participate in the UN system in four ways. They raise issues, such as women's rights and the environment, which then get placed on the world's agendas. They shape decisions taken by the UN, though it can be said that they are much less influential in politics than in the social and humanitarian fields. They enter into partnership with the UN to help carry out its objectives and programs in the field. Finally, they serve as important watchdogs of the UN, observing, criticising and reporting on its role.

Our Class Charter

Name _____

1   At school there are sometimes arguments between children. These arguments can leave children upset or hurt. Discuss the different things which can cause arguments. Write these down in a list. How could you try to prevent these arguments? Would it be easy?

2   Use this Charter to write a set of rules for your class to help all the children to avoid quarrels and work together. You can use the ideals of the United Nations to help you.

Our Class Charter

1   ....
     ....

2   ....
     ....

3   ....
     ....

4   ....
     ....

5   ....
     ....

UN Factfile: The United Nations Charter

For hundreds of years people have thought about how wars between nations could be avoided, by getting them to talk over their differences and settle them that way rather than by fighting. Many schemes for doing this have been suggested, particularly following wars which have caused great casualties and suffering.

Soon after the end of the Second World War (1939-45), the United Nations was set up as an organization for maintaining peace. 51 states signed its Charter. By 24 October, 1945, these governments had confirmed their commitment to the world organization and on that day the United Nations came into existence. This day is now celebrated each year throughout the world as United Nations day.

The main purpose of the United Nations is to stop countries preparing for and fighting wars, but it is not easy. The United Nations does not want countries to fight or people to suffer. In March 1995, there were 185 countries which were members of the United Nations. They have a set of rules called the Charter which everyone can understand and which makes working together easier.

When a country joins the United Nations it has to agree to obey the following rules:

- All Member States are equal
- All Member States must obey the Charter
- Countries must try to settle their differences by peaceful means
- Countries must avoid using force or threatening to use force
- The United Nations may not interfere with the domestic affairs of any country
- Countries should try to assist the United Nations.

The aims of the United Nations
- To keep peace throughout the world
- To develop friendly relations between nations
- To work together to help poor people live better lives, to remove poverty, disease and illiteracy in the world, to stop environmental destruction and to encourage respect for each other's rights and freedoms

 Extension activities

1   Read the Preamble to the Charter (*Resource Point E*). Ask children to compare their charter with the UN Charter. They can write down three similarities and three differences.

2   Using the *Factfile*, ask the children to study the UN rules. What do those rules mean to behaviour at school? Rewrite them as school rules. Who and what do these protect? What kinds of responsibilities go along with them?

3   Ask children to write out some part of the Charter using words they can easily understand.

4   Sit children in groups of no more than six people. Get one child to write down all the concerns that members of the group have about the world. As a group, discuss which are the most important concerns and come to a collective greement on the top three. Put a three next to what the group thinks is the most important, a two by the one that is second most important, and a one beside the concern that is least important to the group. Then think about how you came to agree on these three: did you make convincing arguments and reach a collective decision? did one or two people force them on the group? or did you pick them because an adult or some other person had talked about them? Put together the top three concerns of all the groups in the class. Work out a way to agree to the top four concerns in the class.

5   Identify some recent conflicts. Then discuss their causes. How do these compare to your own arguments or conflicts?

Emblems of the United Nations

Name _____

This is the emblem of the United Nations. It shows the world held in the olive branches of peace.

An emblem can be a badge or a flag. Draw your school emblem in the space provided. If it doesn't have one, design one of your own.

Match the emblems below to each of these United Nations Agencies. Cut out the emblems and names, match them and glue them onto paper.

International Civil Aviation Organization	Food and Agriculture Organization	UN Children's Fund
Centre for Human Rights	World Health Organization	UN High Commissioner for Refugees

UN Factfile: Emblems of the United Nations and Specialised Agencies

An emblem usually has a symbol and possibly letters or words which are easy to recognize. The United Nations has many different departments (agencies) and many have their own emblems.

The Specialised Agencies and some other parts of the UN System have their own emblem to symbolise the work they do.

Art and symbolism are very important in the world of the United Nations. They are a means by which people can express themselves about such powerful ideas as war and peace, love and hate, wealth and poverty. They are also an important means of communicating ideas to people who speak different languages. Sometimes this means writing or painting things which are not very popular.

The United Nations exists to try to bring peace, justice and well-being to our world. There are 185 Member States in the United Nations (March 1995) and many of them like to present the United Nations with a gift – often art or an object that symbolises their culture – when they join or at other important times in the history of their country.

 Extension activities

1   You may wish to photocopy *Starting Point 2* onto A3 paper. Which emblems did the children find difficult to recognise? Ask them to give reasons for this.

2   Ask the children to redesign the emblem they liked least. They should consider if there is anything important to include in their design. The design can be reproduced as a collage, painting or on a computer.

3   Discuss what each of the organizations shown actually does.

4   In groups, design a new school badge. The children must agree on three special things they want to be shown on the badge.

Food and Agriculture Organization

UN High Commissioner for Refugees

Centre for Human Rights

International Civil Aviation Organization

World Health Organization

UN Children's Fund

United We Stand

Name _____

> Read this story with a friend. Then answer the questions below.

Once upon a time there were two men. One was blind and the other was lame. They were walking along together one day when they came to a bad piece of road. It was very bumpy and there were great potholes in it. When the blind man realised what the road was like, he stopped.

"Will you help me over this difficult bit?" he asked the lame man.

"How can I?" asked the lame man. "You know I can't walk properly. My legs are so bad I can hardly get along myself. How can I possibly help you?"

Then he thought about it for a moment. "There is something we could try," he said. "If I climb up on your back, you can carry me. Then I can tell you where to put your feet as we go along. That way, we can use your legs and my eyes together."

They tried it and it worked. The blind man gave the lame man a piggy back over the rough ground and the lame man told the blind man where to tread. That way they both made it across the bad stretch of road.

Questions

1 Do you think this could happen?
2 In the story, the blind man had good legs and the lame man had good eyes. In real life, does everyone have something to give or are some people so badly handicapped that they can't help anyone else?
3 When are the times you have needed someone to help you?

UN Factfile: United Nations

The United Nations is made up of countries that are its members. In March 1995 it had 185 members. It works through Member States discussing and reaching agreement. This is called 'consensus'. Sometimes this is not possible because one or more members disagree. However, when it does act on the basis of agreement it can be very effective. In such circumstances it is greater than the sum of its parts.

Member States have problems in the same way as individuals do. Solving them often means working together. The UN has a number of Specialised Agencies to help countries with their problems. Every member country can choose to pay towards their costs although not every country benefits from their work directly or in the same way.

 Extension activities

Ask the children to consider questions 1 to 5:

1   Have there been times when you have been able to help someone else who badly needed it?

2   How does it feel to be helped? Is it a completely good feeling?

3   How does it feel to help? Does helping sometimes cost you something or stop you doing something you want to do? Now play 'Blind Trust'. Blindfold another student and guide him or her around the class, helping with every task they have to do including drinking water or getting a book. After a few minutes each student should write down how they felt. How do their feelings differ and why? Now answer question 2 again.

4   Do whole families sometimes need help? What sort of help? Who can help them?

5   Do you think whole countries sometimes need help? When does this happen? What sort of help can other countries give them? How do you think they would feel about it?

6   The following games may be started a day or two before reading the story. They are all recommended to promote the ideas of self-esteem and cooperation:

   a   Talking Glasses: This is another circle activity. You need an old pair of sunglasses to pass round. The first child puts the sunglasses on. His/her right hand neighbour then says: "Glasses, glasses say what you see; Tell me what you like best about me." The wearer of the glasses answers for the glasses, says one nice thing about the person who recited the verse, removes the glasses and passes them to his or her left-hand neighbour. The process continues round the circle.

   b   Secret Friends: Print the children's names on small pieces of paper. Fold the pieces of paper and place them in a hat. Begin "Secret Friends" in the morning. Tell the children that they are each going to write a name that they must keep secret. Pass the hat round and ask each child to write the name of a classmate for whom he/she will be a secret friend for the day. Explain that secret friends make an extra effort to be friendly and helpful to the person whose name they have drawn. Towards the end of the day, gather in a circle. Ask the children to take turns in describing friendly things that were done for them throughout the day. Ask each child how this made him/her feel and if he/she can guess who the secret friend is. Were there any negative feelings about being helped?

The Rainbow People

Name _____

Read this story with a friend. List all the things you would need to stay alive. Which colour would you prefer to be?

In the beginning, the world was very still and quiet. The ground seemed to be covered with dull coloured rocks and stones. But if you took a closer look, you could see that they were not stones but tiny people who were not moving at all. One day a wind blew over the land. It warmed the people and filled them with life and with love. They began to move … to look at each other … to speak to each other … to care about each other.

As they explored their world, they found coloured ribbons lying on the ground. They were excited and ran about collecting them up. Some chose blue, some green, some red and some yellow. They enjoyed tying the ribbons round each other and laughing at the bright colours.

Suddenly another wind blew. This time it made them shiver with cold. They looked at each other, realised they looked different … and stopped trusting each other.

- The reds gathered together and ran into a corner.
- The blues gathered together and ran into a corner.
- The greens gathered together and ran into a corner.
- The yellows gathered together and ran into a corner.

They forgot that they had been friends and cared for each other. The other colours just seemed strange and different. They built walls to separate themselves and keep the others out.

But they found that:

- The reds had water but no food.
- The blues had food but no water.
- The greens had twigs to make fire but no shelter.

- The yellows had shelter but nothing to keep them warm.

Suddenly a stranger appeared and stood in the centre of the land. He looked at the people and the walls separating them in amazement, and said loudly, "Come on out everybody. What are you afraid of? Let's talk to each other." The people peeped out at him and slowly came out of their corners into the centre. The stranger said, "Now just tell one another what you have to give and what you need to be given."

The blues said, "We have plenty of food to give but we need water."

The reds said, "We have plenty of water to give but we need food."

The greens said, "We have plenty of wood for fire but we need shelter."

The yellows said, "We have plenty of shelter but we need warmth."

The stranger said, "Why don't you put together what you have and share it? Then you can all have enough to eat, drink, keep warm and have shelter."

They talked and the feeling of love returned. They remembered that they had been friends. They knocked down the walls and welcomed each other as old friends. When they realised that the colours had divided them, they wanted to throw them away. But they knew that they would miss the richness of the bright colours. So instead they mixed the colours to make a beautiful rainbow ribbon. They called themselves the Rainbow People. The rainbow ribbon became their symbol of peace.

Original story by Carolyn Askar

UN Factfile: United Nations Secretary-General

The idealism in this story reflects very closely the idealism in the United Nations Charter – cooperation is better than conflict. The 'stranger' can be likened to the Secretary-General who acts on behalf of the United Nations. The current Secretary-General is Boutros Boutros-Ghali, an Egyptian, who is the sixth person to hold this position. The others have been:

Trygve Lie of Norway	1946-53
Dag Hammarskjöld of Sweden	1953-61
U Thant of Burma (now Myanmar)	1961-71
Kurt Waldheim of Austria	1972-81
Javier Pérez de Cuéllar of Peru	1982-91

The Secretary-General can bring to the attention of the Security Council any matter which, in his opinion, threatens international peace. Nonetheless, it is up to the Security Council to authorise him to take action. He cannot decide on action on his own or without the approval of the Security Council.

The Secretary-General is also head of the UN Secretariat which numbers more than 15 000 men and women from over 150 different countries. They take an oath not to seek or receive instructions from any government or outside authority. Under Article 100 of the United Nations Charter, the Member States undertake not to seek to influence them in their work. The Secretary-General is appointed by the General Assembly on the recommendation of Security-Council. It is customary that the person appointed is not from a country which is a Permanent Member of the Security Council. These Permanent Members are China, France, Russian Federation, the United Kingdom and the US.

If this is organized as a role-play, do leave time to discuss as a class at the end and give the children an opportunity to get out of role before they leave you.

Extension activities

1   On the first day organize the class to act this out. Get them to choose which colour they would like to be and why. Ask them to bring in anything that is their chosen colour for the next day including clothes. The reds should bring buckets or other receptacles for their water; the blues should bring baskets for their food; the greens should bring sticks and twigs; and the yellows should bring umbrellas or pieces of cardboard for their shelter. Act it out again having got them to choose who should be the 'stranger'. They should then perform an assembly for other classes.

2   Ask the class to elect a Secretary-General for the week. He or she would act to settle any matters of dispute between members of the class. This might be something to do with bullying, an argument or someone who has broken a school rule. The person elected would have to have the full support of the class so the teacher may wish to use a system of transferable voting rather than simply counting up total votes for each person.

   Candidates would have to be nominated and seconded; they would have to accept the nomination; they would have to say what they would try to do and how they would do it. The class would then vote in order of preference. If no candidate had more votes than all the others put together, then the last placed person would be eliminated. The second choice votes on these ballot papers are then counted and so on. An alternative would be to give the class two days to come up with a name acceptable to everyone – this is how it is done by the Security Council.

3   Write out a job description that the Security Council might give to a new Secretary-General. It should state a) the jobs he or she would have to do, and b) the skills he or she would need to be a good mediator. Would you like such a job? Before you decide make a list of all the good things about the job and all the bad things.

Cooperation is Better than Conflict

Name _____

Cut out the strips below and arrange them in an order which shows that cooperation is better than conflict. The top strip is the first one, but the others are in the wrong order. Remember, the donkeys are trying to eat the hay.

UN Factfile: United Nations Security Council

The United Nations was originally set up in 1945 *"to save succeeding generations from the scourge of war which twice in our lifetime has brought untold sorrow to mankind ....."*. The horrors of the Second World War served to remind people, including politicians and world leaders, what price was paid through conflict rather than cooperation.

The Security Council was empowered under the Charter to maintain world peace and security. It can investigate and provide mediation in any international dispute which may threaten world peace; it can recommend action which may include economic sanctions or military action against an aggressor. It also has the power to formulate plans for the establishment of a system to regulate armaments. It has 15 members, five of which are permanent – China, France, Russian Federation, the UK and the US. Any one of these states may veto a decision of the Security Council. The other 10 members are elected by the General Assembly for two-year terms taking care to ensure that each region of the world is represented. All countries which are members of the United Nations must follow the decisions of the Security Council.

Extension activities

The aim of *Starting Point 5* is for children to realise that most tasks can be made much easier if people work together rather than in opposition. The appropriate order for the pictures is given on the right.

1   Instead of having students piece the puzzle together individually, the teacher can make copies of the strips and give one strip to each student. Then students would have to go around looking at other students' strips and eventually cooperate with the other five people who have a piece of the series to put the sequence together.

   a   Each group should explain to the rest of the class why they decided on their particular order.

   b   Children can be asked to write their own account of how they came to cooperate in ordering the sequence. Were there any problems? How would they act differently to make things go smoother next time?

2   Using Music and Dance, the teacher could lead sessions on aggressive moves and sounds as opposed to softer, more harmonious sounds. The children could be given a selection of instruments and/or movements and be asked to communicate a message to their group or the rest of the class.

3   Using *Resource Point J*, decorate your classroom with paper doves – symbols of peace.

4   In pairs, children might be asked to think of situations at home or school where they have used cooperation rather than confrontation. In pairs, one child would act as the listener who asks questions for clarification, the other would explain their chosen situation. After a given time they should change roles. Ask the students what they have learned from this exercise. Are there any responsibilities that go with cooperating or trying to avoid conflict? What would they be?

One Thousand Paper Cranes

Name _____

Read this with a friend and talk about it.

In 1945, towards the end of the Second World War, the first atomic bomb (A-bomb) was dropped on the city of Hiroshima in Japan. The city was destroyed and many thousands of people were killed. Although the bomb was hundreds of times more powerful than an ordinary bomb, it had something else which ordinary bombs did not have – radiation. We know that radiation is very dangerous and can cause diseases such as cancer.

A young Japanese girl called Sadako was living just one and a half miles from Hiroshima when the bomb exploded, but she was not burned or injured as far as anyone could see. Yet ten years later, after Hiroshima had been rebuilt, she became ill with leukemia – a cancer of the blood – and had to stay in hospital. She was scared, very scared; she knew she could die. Her family and friends visited her every day to try and cheer her up.

Her best friend, Chizuko, told her the story of the crane which is a sacred bird in Japan. The crane was thought to live for thousands of years and if a sick person folds a thousand paper cranes, then that person will get better.

Sadako decided to fold a thousand cranes. Day after day she continued folding and she found that doing this was a good way of feeling braver. Sometimes she was too ill to fold many cranes, but she still tried. When Sadako's family and friends visited her in the hospital, she tried to keep smiling and happy so they would not worry too much.

Sadako managed to fold over six hundred cranes but she did not get better. She continued patiently to fold more cranes, but sadly she finally died. She had folded six hundred and forty-four paper cranes.

Sadako's classmates decided to fold the remaining three hundred and fifty-six cranes and all one thousand were buried with her.

Sadako was not the only child to die of leukemia in Hiroshima. Lots of other children had died or were dying of leukemia. (It was known as the A-bomb disease.)

A club was formed by the children to raise money for a monument to Sadako. The club grew and thousands of schools all over the world gave money. After three years they had enough money to pay for the monument. It is called the Children's Peace Monument and it stands in the Peace Park in Hiroshima. A message is carved into the stone:

This is our cry,
This is our prayer;
Peace in the World.

UN Factfile: United Nations and Disarmament

The UN Charter states *"We the peoples of the United Nations determined to save succeeding generations from the scourge of war, which twice in our lifetime has brought untold sorrow to mankind…"*.

The horrors and sufferings of the Second World War persuaded many countries that it was essential to set up an organization which would help to prevent war in the future.

Much of its work since that time has been devoted to disarmament, particularly the control and dismantling of nuclear weapons. It has a Disarmament Commission which reports annually to the General Assembly with recommendations for specific action. There is also a Conference on Disarmament composed of 40 members including the five nuclear-weapon states. Since 1959 the goal of all disarmament initiatives has been *"general and complete disarmament"*. The UN

has had limited but important successes including:

The *Antarctic Treaty* in 1959, which was the first treaty to create a nuclear weapon free zone; the *Partial Test-Ban Treaty* of 1963 outlawed nuclear tests in the atmosphere and outer space; and in 1969 the *Non-Proliferation Treaty* was agreed in order to prevent the spread of nuclear technology from nuclear to non-nuclear states.

Work continues on the development of a comprehensive nuclear test-ban treaty and agreements to control the development, spread and use of chemical weapons.

The International Atomic Energy Agency (IAEA) is involved in monitoring, verification and the peaceful uses of nuclear technology.

Extension activities

1   The true story overleaf is sad but also full of hope. Children should read the story and with a friend try to find the hopes there are. Tell them that there is now 'The Paper Crane Club' in Hiroshima where members look after the monument. They visit survivors of the A-bomb who are getting old or sick or just need help. They also fold paper cranes. Sometimes the cranes are hung on the monument or given to sick people to cheer them up. Others are given to visitors to Hiroshima to remind them of what happened there. Children could find Japan on a map of the world (*Resource Point F*) and then, on a map of Japan, find and label Hiroshima.

2   'The Paper Crane Club' is an example of how children can get involved and make a difference. Children could find local memorials, parks, or statues dedicated to peace and research into them. Ask children to design their own Peace Monument.

3   What does 'peace' mean to you? The African-American pacifist Martin Luther King Jr said peace is not just "the absence of tensions", it is "the presence of justice." What to you think he meant by that? Think of examples in your own life where there has been no visible conflict, but there was no justice either. In groups come up with ways you would have changed them. In groups, the children can make a 'group statue' by using their bodies. The statue should represent 'peace'. They could also try making a similar statue to represent 'war'. Either the teacher can photograph them or someone in the class could draw the statue.

4   Use *Resource Sheet I* to make a paper crane. Organize an assembly for the school and tell them all about Sadako. Children could act out the story. Give everyone a paper crane and ask them to display it somewhere in the school during the day. Children could even be asked to give the paper crane to someone in the school with whom they would like to make peace.

The Little Flecked Hen

Name _____

> Read the following story. Then get into groups of four: one of you will be the hen, one the rat, one the dog and one the goose. What is the moral of this story?

Once upon a time there was a little hen with brown wings and a brown and cream flecked body. She lived, with her five chicks, in the country and they ate what they could find and also food the little flecked hen grew herself. One day the little flecked hen found some grains of wheat. She knew she could plant them and grow more wheat to eat, so she asked people to help her.

"Who will help me plant my grains of wheat?" asked the little flecked hen.

"Not I," said the goose, "but I'll sell you some coffee bushes. You'll make lots of money if you grow coffee instead of wheat."

"Not I," said the dog, "but I'll buy the coffee from you when you've grown it."

"Not I," said the rat, "but I'll lend you the money you need to start with."

So the little flecked hen planted her land with coffee instead of wheat.

"Who will help me grow this coffee?" asked the little flecked hen.

"Not I," said the goose, "but I'll sell you some fertilizer to help it to grow."

"Not I," said the dog, "but I'll sell you some pesticides to keep it free from disease."

"Not I," said the rat, "but I'll lend you the money to buy the fertilizer and the pesticides you need."

So the little flecked hen worked long and hard. She spread the fertilizer and sprayed the insecticide on her coffee bushes. Even though it was costing her much more than it would have done to grow wheat for herself, she kept thinking of the money she would get for the coffee and of what she could buy with the money.

Then came harvest time.

"Who will help me to sell my coffee?" asked the little flecked hen.

"Not I," said the goose, "but you will need my factory to roast and pack it. You can pay me to use it."

"Not I," said the dog. "Everyone is growing coffee now and the price has fallen. In fact it has hit rock bottom!"

"Not I," said the rat, "but you will have to pay back the money you have borrowed now and the interest as well."

Then the little flecked hen realised that she had made a mistake in growing coffee instead of wheat, because she was deep in debt and had nothing for herself and her chicks to eat.

"Who will help me find something to eat?" asked the little flecked hen.

"Not I," said the goose. "You haven't any money to pay for it."

"Not I," said the dog. "There's not enough food to go round since everyone started to grow coffee."

"Not I," said the rat, "but I'll take over your land to make up for the money you owe and perhaps I'll let you stay and work for me."

UN Factfile: Food and Agriculture Organization of the United Nations (FAO)

The FAO was founded at a conference in Quebec on 16 October 1945. Since 1979, that date has been observed annually as World Food Day.

The aims of FAO are to raise levels of nutrition and standards of living, to improve production, processing, marketing and the distribution of all food and agricultural products from farms, forests and fisheries: to promote rural development and improve the living conditions of rural populations; and, by these means, to eliminate hunger.

FAO also sponsors the World Food Programme which uses food, cash and services from Member States to support programmes of social and economic development as well as to provide relief in emergency situations.

Its work is concerned with seed production, soil protection, conservation, the sensible use of fertilizers and forest resources, with animal diseases (such as trypanosomiasis – sleeping sickness – in Africa) and land reform. It promotes the use of renewable sources of energy, marine and inland fisheries.

An important part of its work is its Global Information and Early Warning System which provides up-to-date information on the world food situation and identifies countries threatened by shortages. Potential donors are then able to make more informed decisions on where best to target their help.

The material in this sheet is based on FAO's publication *Protect and Produce – Putting the pieces together.*

World Food Day is 16 October.

Address: FAO, Via delle Terme di Caracalla, 1-00100 Rome, Italy.

Extension activities

1   Children should read the story to themselves or in groups. In groups, ask the children to act out the story. They will need people to be the hen, the goose, the dog and the rat. They will also need sacks or bags for the fertilizer, the insecticide and the seed and some paper for money. Check that they have understood difficult words/concepts eg fertilizer, pesticides, interest, falling prices (for the seller as well as for the buyer), cash crop etc.

2   Discuss possible sequels to the story. For example, did the little flecked hen stay and work for the rat? If not, where did she go, how did she live? If so, what happened next season? Improvise and add this sequel to the play.

3   This exercise will help you understand how your community works. Divide into groups. One group can look at what energy and resources are used by your community (electricity, water, etc), where it comes from and how it is distributed; another group can do the same thing for goods like food and refrigerators; and another group can look at people's occupations, what proportion works in agriculture, factories, commerce, government, and what it is they do for the community (eg make water available, etc). Then get together and draw a large map of how your community works to meet its needs. What would happen if suddenly all connection with the outside world was cut off?

Shipwrecked!

Name _____

Map of .... Island

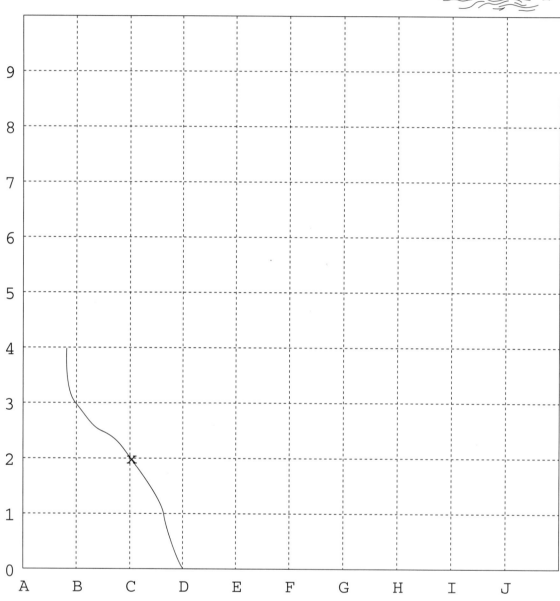

You have been washed ashore at C2. You can see along the shore for some distance and this has been marked on your map for you. Your first task is to explore the island and complete the map. Plot on the following coordinates:

B4, B7, C8, D8, E7, F8, G9, H8, H7, G6, F4, G3, H4, I3, I2, H1, G1, F2, E1 and remember it is an island so use curved lines. Decide on a name for your island and discuss what you will need to survive. Using coloured pencils and a key put some of these needs on your island: a river, forest and hills. Then decide on the best place for your camp.

UN Factfile: Universal Declaration of Human Rights

On 10 December 1948, the General Assembly of the United Nations adopted and proclaimed the Universal Declaration of Human Rights. It has set the standard for human rights ever since and is used extensively by human rights groups such as Amnesty International when campaigning for countries to improve their human rights standards.

The declaration states that everyone is born free and equal, and should not be mistreated due to their political views, religion, gender, nationality or race. Now, there is also a similar declaration that protects the rights of children (see *Resource Point G*).

Article 25 states *(1) Everyone has the right to a standard of living adequate for the health and well-being of himself and of his family, including food, clothing, housing and medical care and necessary social services, and the right to security in the event of unemployment, sickness, disability, widowhood, old age or other lack of livelihood in circumstances beyond his control.*

Many countries have incorporated it into their constitutions.

 ## Extension activities

1   Imagine you are alone on the island. Describe how you would survive for a very long time by using the resources you have around you. For example, you would fish, or grow fruit and vegetables or even find some animals to keep. You can draw these on your map, indicating fishing areas and agricultural areas.

2   Now get in groups with a fresh map, with all the resources like mountains, rivers, fruit trees, etc, marked on it. Divide the island among yourselves and draw the borders. You still need to survive for a very long time, but there are other people with their own territories. Your attitude to begin with should be to have as much as possible without regard for others. Discuss what would happen on the island.

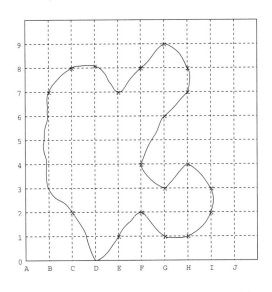

3   Now change attitudes. Your goal should be to make sure everyone on the island has as much as possible. What would you have to do? How are the actions and behaviours in these two scenarios different?

4   What would happen if one territory was richer or stronger than the others and so did not want to cooperate because it thought it could get everything it wanted anyway?

5   Based on what you have learned from these three scenarios, write a set of rules that would ensure that no matter what attitude each territory had the others would still be treated fairly. That is what the UN tries to do and you can use the *Factfile* for guidance.

6   Imagine what would happen in your community if everyone wanted to have their own way. What could happen? Who would be getting their way and how? Now think of ways of not letting this happen. How might this Ethiopian proverb help: *When spider webs unite, they can bind a lion.*

7   Are there a set of rules in your community, written or not, that help people be fair?

A Refugee's Day

Name _____

Work with a friend to find out how much time the refugee spends eating, route planning, travelling, sleeping, washing dishes or washing herself. Then complete the pie chart. Use different colours for each activity.

A refugee's day

06.00	Get up
06.00 - 6.15	Wash and dress
06.15 - 6.30	Fold away bedding
06.30 - 7.00	Breakfast
07.00 - 7.30	Wash dishes
07.30 - 12.00	Travel
12.00 - 12.30	Lunch
12.30 - 13.00	Wash dishes
13.00 - 13.30	Sleep or rest
13.30 - 18.00	Travel
18.00 - 18.30	Supper
18.30 - 19.00	Wash dishes
19.00 - 19.30	Rest
19.30 - 21.00	Plan route for following day
21.00 - 21.15	Washing
21.15 - 21.30	Get bedding out
21.30	Sleep

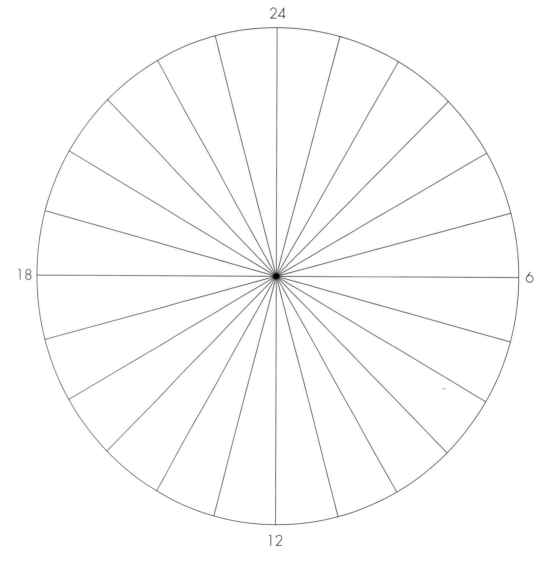

UN Factfile: United Nations High Commissioner for Refugees

Who is a refugee?

The 1951 Convention and the 1967 Protocol relating to the Status of Refugees define a refugee as a person who, *"owing to a well-founded fear of persecution for reasons of race, religion, nationality, membership of a particular social group or political opinion, is outside the country of his nationality and is unable or, owing to such fear, is unwilling to avail himself of the protection of that country..."*

There are over 20 million refugees in the world today. Most are women and children; all were forced by intolerance and violence to flee into exile. They are from every race and religion; they come from every part of the globe. Few countries have been spared the tragedy of refugees. Their numbers grow each year, a sign of continuing upheaval around the world. Assistance to these refugees is the responsibility of the United Nations High Commissioner for Refugees (UNHCR).

What does UNHCR do?

First and foremost, UNHCR's task is to protect refugees and to intervene with governments on their behalf. After the Second World War, the international community was faced, even more acutely than after the First World War, with the problem of millions of refugees and displaced persons in Europe. UNHCR was created by the United Nations General Assembly to help these people and to find lasting solutions to their plight. UNHCR began its operations on 1 January 1951, initially for a three year period. Since then, despite remarkable achievements, refugee flows have continued unabated, and the Office's mandate has repeatedly been renewed.

Chief, Public Information, UNHCR, Case Postale 2500, CH-1211, Geneva 2 Dépôt, Switzerland.

Refugees are often seen as burdens, people who need help but cannot give very much. However, each refugee has the potential to make exceptional contributions to their new countries and to humanity. Did you know that several refugees have been awarded the Nobel Peace Prize? Rigoberta Menchu, the Mayan Indian activist from Guatemala, received it in 1992; and Willy Brandt, a German who escaped to Denmark and Norway and later returned to Germany, received it in 1971. Did you know that Albert Einstein was also a refugee? Find out more about these people or other famous people who were refugees.

 ### Extension activities

1   Children could record how they spend their day and fill in a copy of the pie chart. Compare it to that of the refugee. Discuss how this daily routine might be different in a) a war zone, b) a drought stricken area. Draw pie charts for a day in the life of a refugee in each of these situations.

2   Find some recent news reports about refugees. Collect as much information as possible about them and the region they came from. Why did they move? How are they living now? Are there any international organizations helping them?

3   Give out copies of *Resource Point G* The UN Convention on the Rights of the Child. Ask the children to imagine they are a refugee child. Which of their rights will they have lost?

4   Find out if there are any organizations in your area that help newcomers. Visit the organization and report on what they do. Who are the people who go there? Who works there? How do they help out?

Leaving Home

Name _____

1

I'm from a village in Brazil. The harvest was poor last year, so I have brought my family to Rio de Janeiro for a better way of life.

2

When the war began in Bosnia, we managed to get out. We are now living safely in Germany.

3

I'm a guest worker. I work in a car factory in Holland. My family live in Tunisia and I send them money each month.

4

Twenty years ago, I left Britain to seek a better life in Australia. I have a good job and lifestyle to match it.

5

My family left Bangladesh four years ago. The floods ruined our crops and destroyed our homes. We escaped to Britain.

Migration is when people move from one place to another. Discuss with a friend why people should wish to move. Look at the speech bubbles on the left of this page. Some of these people have chosen to move. This is called *voluntary migration*. Others have had to move – this is called *forced migration*. Discuss with your friend which is which, cut them out and sort them into two piles. One for "voluntary" and one for "forced" repatriation.

People usually move in order to improve their quality of life. Look at the speech bubbles on the right of this page. Discuss with a friend if their quality of life has improved or not.

6

I work for a newspaper, on the sports page. My company have trained me and paid for evening classes.

7

We feel happy here. Before we fled away, we were frightened for our lives. Things are much better now.

8

I have started my own small printing business. We print posters. I employ three people in my firm.

9

We left our country for a better life. Since we have arrived here, we have had to suffer a lot of racism. We are afraid.

10

We both work in a clothes factory. We work long hours for a very low pay. It is not fair.

UN Factfile: United Nations Centre for Human Settlements (HABITAT)

Migrants from rural areas usually head for cities in the hope of finding jobs and a better quality of life. This has been one of the major causes of urbanisation in both the industrialised and developing countries.

HABITAT was established in 1978 with its headquarters in Nairobi, Kenya. It acts as a focal point for developments in the field of human settlements and is particularly committed to action which improves shelter for the poor. HABITAT also coordinates human settlement activities within the United Nations System.

Areas of work include urban and regional planning, rural and urban housing, slum upgrading, low-cost building technology and urban and rural water supply and sanitation. Its Urban Management Programme (in conjunction with the UN Development Programme and the World Bank) aims to improve urban efficiency and living conditions for the poor. In 1990 it added an environmental arm to the Programme in order to help address such issues in the cities and towns of developing countries.

In the same year the Centre launched the Sustainable Cities Programme which was intended to support municipal authorities and their public and private sector partners with regard to environmental planning.

World HABITAT Day is observed in every Member State on the first Monday of October each year.

For further information contact; HABITAT, Room M-337, PO Box 30030, Nairobi, Kenya.

Extension activities

1   Encourage children to work in small groups. This activity is meant to encourage discussion about *voluntary* and *forced migration* and whether or not the ensuing quality of life is better or worse.

2   Why do people move? Ask children to use newspaper and television items to give examples eg Bosnia, Rwanda, Cambodia, Bangladesh, Turkey etc. You probably know someone who has moved from another town or another country. Think about them and write down why you think they moved and how they feel about their old and new homes. Then talk to them and ask them about these things. Is what they told you different from what you had thought? In what ways?

3   Write a diary of a day in the life of a migrant recently arrived in a new country. The children should be encouraged to choose one of the people described in *Starting Point 10*. How might local people help them to settle in and feel part of the community?

4   Put the following scenario to a group of children or the whole class, if necessary. As the UN Habitat Representative in the capital city of a developing country, you have been asked to make recommendations for improving the housing problem. In short, there are not enough houses to cope with the influx of migrants from the countryside. Present your thoughts by completing this table:

Problem	Solution	Priority out of 10 with 1 being top priority
Slums on the edge of city		
Overcrowded housing near city centre		
Congested public transport		
Poor water supply		
Racism		

What do You Think about the Environment?

Name _____

Read the following passage and draw a picture of what it describes, especially in the italicised phrases.

Use arrows to show what is happening.

Pollution in rivers can be caused in many different ways. *Fumes from cars and power stations* mix with *water vapour* to form *acid rain*. Some farmers use *chemical sprays and fertilizers* on their crops and these may drain into *rivers*. Carelessness can cause pollution. *Factories and sewage treatment plants* are supposed to treat their waste products but accidents can happen. If chemical waste from factories is not safely disposed of, *toxins can drain into the rivers*.

Which of these do you think is happening to rivers, lakes or the sea in your area?

_____

_____

_____

_____

UN Factfile: UNESCO – Man and the Biosphere Programme

UNESCO came into being on 4 November 1946. Its main aim is to contribute to peace and security in the world by promoting collaboration among nations through education, science, culture and communication.

For education, it seeks to provide basic education for all by training teachers, planners and administrators; for culture, one of its priorities is to preserve national cultural values and heritage; and in the area of communication it encourages a freer and wider flow of information without obstructing freedom of expression.

For science, it seeks to improve the management of the environment and to make better use of its natural resources. In 1968, UNESCO convened the Biosphere Conference which, for more or less the first time, called together the international scientific community in order to tell governments that the environment was in bad shape and getting worse. Biosphere is simply the air and water in which we and the animals live. The UNESCO conference emphasised the need to treat the biosphere as a whole and that human beings were integral to it.

In 1971, UNESCO launched the *Man and the Biosphere (MAB) Programme* in order to seek answers to how humanity was affecting the biosphere and what could be done to avoid further degradation.

For further information on MAB, write to:
UNESCO
75352 Paris 07SP
France

 Extension activities

1   a   Discuss: What is the environment? What makes it up? What do we get from it and why is it important to us?
    b   Working with a partner, children should discuss the things that they like and dislike about the environment.
    c   Then, using a flashlight, they should take it in turns to light up the profile of their partner's head and cast a shadow onto a large piece of plain paper and draw around the outline. The result should be two outlines with the faces looking at each other.
    d   Each pair can then add pictures and words between their faces to show the things that they like and dislike about the environment, as discussed in 1b.
    e   Each child can add pictures and words to their own head outline to show their favourite things in the environment.

2   a   Children could think about their own activities during the day. Do they do anything that may be damaging or polluting the air, water or earth? Make a list of these and propose how they might be able to change them. Now make a list of everything they see outside. Which of these could be replaced quickly, if at all, if they were damaged?
    b   Children could discuss how they can tell people about what they are destroying and how they can make them listen and act.

3   Children could do one or more of the following special tasks: plant acorns or any other plant choosing sites carefully and dedicating them to people whom you respect; organize a public speaking or song writing about the environment.

4   UNESCO gathered scientists from all around the world to tell governments that the environment is in danger. What do you think can result from such a conference? Why would you expect governments or individuals to listen to UNESCO?

Pollution

Name _____

Water is one of the most important resources in our lives. We all need water to survive. But if water is polluted we cannot use it.

The following sentences are to do with water pollution. Use the six words listed below to complete the sentences:

malaria   sanitation   contaminated   filter   cholera   stagnant

1 Diseases such as .... can be easily spread through contact with

    .... water.

2 Other diseases like .... are passed through infection-carrying

    insects which breed in .... water. In some countries poor

    .... is the cause.

3 We can make sure that our water is clean and safe. Using a proper water

    .... can help a lot.

UN Factfile: United Nations Convention on the Law of the Sea

In 1958 the United Nations first considered the question "Who owns the sea?". In 1969, the General Assembly unanimously accepted a Declaration of Principles, which stated that *"the sea-bed and ocean floor, …as well as the resources of the area are the common heritage of mankind"*. These areas were to be reserved for peaceful purposes and not subject to national jurisdiction. Exploring or exploiting these areas was only to be allowed with the permission of an International Seabed Authority.

There are many issues that have to be considered including fishing rights, cabling, transit by foreign ships, overflight by aircraft, scientific research, pollution and conservation. It has been agreed that coastal countries, or countries bordering on water, have exclusive rights to fish or use the sea for other economic purposes up to 200 nautical miles from their coast. Beyond that, no one country has exclusive rights to the sea, and activities beyond that area are monitored by the International Seabed Authority. This was done in part to prevent destructive activities like overfishing and polluting the sea. It also gives land-locked countries the chance to use the seas for transport and fishing.

The Convention was opened for signature in 1982 and 117 States signed on the first day – more than any treaty had ever before received on its first day. Within two years 159 States had signed. States are then required to ratify it and it was agreed that the Convention would come into force one year after the sixtieth state had so ratified. The convention entered into force on 16 November 1994.

The correct order for completing the sentences is as follows: cholera, contaminated, malaria, stagnant, sanitation, filter.

Extension activities

1   Children could experiment with making their own water filter to find which materials are most efficient. Suggested resources are as follows: large, clear plastic bottle (with bottom cut off and turned upside down), clear container (to collect water), filter paper, gravel, sand, mesh colander, nylon tights etc. An example is shown in the diagram on the right.

2   Usable water needs to be saved so we can all keep using it. List those of your daily activities that use up water. Which of these is basic to your survival and which could be considered a luxury? How else does water get wasted? Design a poster for your home to encourage people to save water.

3   How would your way of life change if you had to live on less water? Try measuring out about 6 litres of water and only use that for the next 24 hours. Report on your experience.

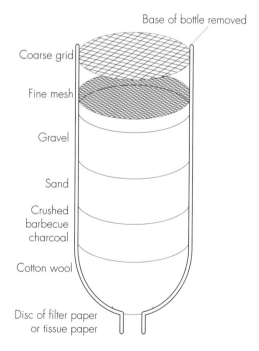

Base of bottle removed

Coarse grid

Fine mesh

Gravel

Sand

Crushed barbecue charcoal

Cotton wool

Disc of filter paper or tissue paper

How to Be a Recycler

Name _____

Power station

Why should we recycle?

The rich countries of the world use huge amounts of fossil fuels such as gas, coal and oil. The fuels are used to make electricity which heats homes, lights streets and fuels cars. These fossil fuels are resources which are not equally shared. The USA has only 6% of the world's population, but it uses 30% of the world's energy. India has almost 20% of the world's population but uses only 2% of the energy.

We can help in our own small way at home. We can recycle fabrics, papers, metals, plastics and glass. When you recycle you are not using new products which need fresh supplies of precious fossil fuels. We can also remember to switch off lights and turn off the taps to conserve electricity and water.

Here is an idea for recycling. In order to be a recycler you will need a notebook.

1 Get some scrap paper (computer paper or paper used only on one side).
2 Find some stiff card (from shoe boxes, new shirts or cereal packets).
3 Get an old shoelace, string or plastic thread.
4 Put them together like this.

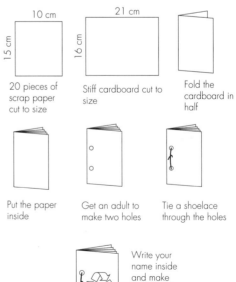

10 cm
15 cm
20 pieces of scrap paper cut to size

21 cm
16 cm
Stiff cardboard cut to size

Fold the cardboard in half

Put the paper inside

Get an adult to make two holes

Tie a shoelace through the holes

Write your name inside and make notes of all your recycling information

UN Factfile: United Nations Environment Programme (UNEP)

The United Nations has pioneered the concept of sustainable development – economic and social progress which can be supported without damaging the life chances of future generations. The concept of the 'global commons' and of global equality are also important here. The global commons are such things as the air, the sea, the forests, water – the common heritage of mankind.

At the forefront of these ideas is the United Nations Environment Programme which is based in Nairobi, Kenya – the first UN Agency to be based in a developing country. Its main aim is to promote environmental action and awareness worldwide. For example, it sponsors and carries out projects that develop a country's energy resources without harming the environment.

It also operates the Global Environment Monitoring System (GEMS) across 142 countries. This involves monitoring the atmosphere and climate, the oceans, renewable terrestrial resources and trans-boundary pollution including impact on health. It also coordinates the environmental activities of all UN agencies.

World Environment Day is 5 June.

For further information write to Chief, Information Service, UNEP, PO Box 30552, Nairobi, Kenya.

Extension activities

1   What resources, like water, gas, or electricity are used in your schools and classrooms? What are they used for? Can other sources of energy give you the same uses?

2   Everything we use comes from our environment. Producing them uses up valuable resources and energy. Sometimes we throw out things like bags or bottles very quickly. Of all the things you use during the day, which can be re-used? Which do you actually re-use? Keep a daily list of the things you re-used; state what they were, and what you re-used them for. See if by the end of a month or two you can increase their number *and* their uses. Share your ideas with your classmates so that the whole class can recycle more.

3   Make a list of ways in which you or your community recycle and re-use materials. Are there any organized efforts to recycle, such as garbage projects or bins for plastic containers or paper? Find out about these if you can: how did they start? What do they do? Set up recycling projects in class. For example, you can keep a box for all the waste paper. Instead of throwing it all out, see what you can do with it. Can you re-use the paper for art projects or for taking notes? You can have other boxes for cloth or plastic.

4   In groups or as a whole class play out this scenario. A reporter has revealed that there is a plan to turn an area of the city, including some houses and a field or a park, into a highway in order to cut down congestion in an already crowded city centre. Each student should assume a role: the reporter, the Head of the Traffic Department, the City's Chief Health Officer, the mayor, a judge, a family who will have to be moved, an environmentalist. First think carefully about what your position would be: should the city go ahead with the plan or cancel it? There could be very good arguments for both sides. Present arguments to the judge who will have to decide whether the highway will be built or not.

5   Now try and think about the environment globally. How might what you do or use at home affect the environment in another country? Write a letter to the Executive Director of UNEP outlining your concerns about the environment and what you think can be done to solve the problems.

The Rainforests

Name _____

A rainforest is a tropical forest with a large rainfall. Rainforests are being destroyed at an alarming rate. In the last 50 years almost half of the rainforests of the world have been destroyed. Discuss the statements with a friend. Carefully cut out the shapes and put them together to make a simple tree. It describes some of the reasons given for keeping the rainforests.

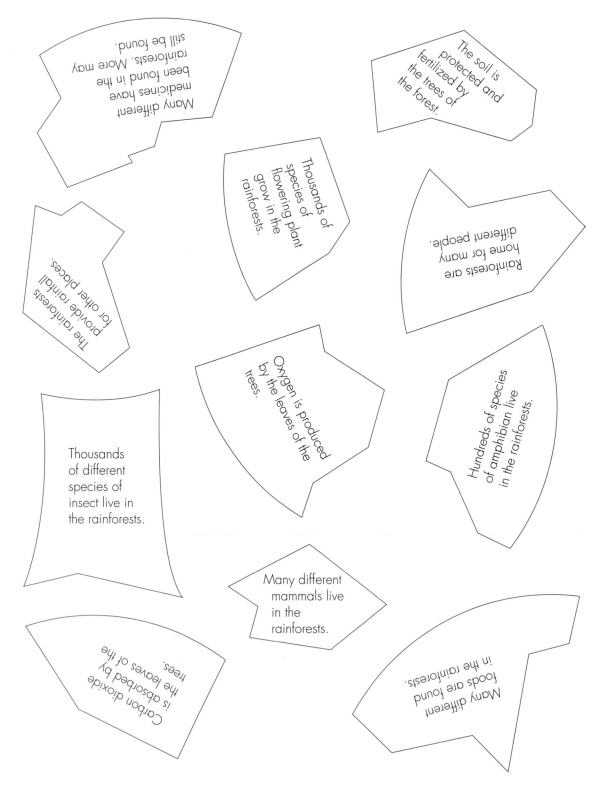

Many different medicines have been found in the rainforests. More may still be found.

The soil is protected and fertilized by the trees of the forest.

Thousands of species of flowering plant grow in the rainforests.

Rainforests are home for many different people.

The rainforests provide rainfall for other places.

Oxygen is produced by the leaves of the trees.

Hundreds of species of amphibian live in the rainforests.

Thousands of different species of insect live in the rainforests.

Many different mammals live in the rainforests.

Carbon dioxide is absorbed by the leaves of the trees.

Many different foods are found in the rainforests.

UN Factfile: United Nations Environment Programme (UNEP)

UNEP believes it is vital to save the world's tropical rainforest – now disappearing at the rate of nearly an acre a second or 3000 acres an hour. They cover 6% of the Earth's land surface and are the source of half of our medicines. They regulate climate and prevent floods and landslides. UNEP encourages sustainable development of the tropical forests. They are an important resource not only for us but the indigenous peoples who live there. They are also home to the great majority of living species.

Rainforests are cleared by people. They are logged for timber to make such things as furniture; they are cleared for cattle ranches so that we can obtain beef; they are flooded when dams are constructed to provide electricity for towns; they are destroyed to make way for roads and mining; they are cut down to provide building materials and fuel for local people; they are cleared and burned to provide farmland.

UNEP ensured that environmental considerations were part of the International Tropical Timber Agreement which regulates the trade in timber. They have also helped develop the Tropical Forestry Action Plan. A key issue is how to compensate countries with rainforests in order to help them protect the natural wealth that their forests represent.

Further information on UNEP can be obtained from Chief, Information Service, UNEP, PO Box 30552, Nairobi, Kenya.

You may wish to photocopy *Starting Point 14* on to A3 paper. The tree should look like this when completed.

Extension activities

1   Using *Starting Point 14*, children can, in groups, pick out four shapes which they think contain the most important aspects of the rainforest and two which contain the least important. They should give reasons for both and compare their decisions with another group.

2   Discuss basic needs (eg water, food, shelter, warmth etc) and draw a poster to show how the forest provides these for those who live in the forest (indigenous peoples). How do you think rainforests contribute to your lives, even if you do not live in or near them?

3   Turn the classroom into a rainforest. Use carpet tubes and cover with brown paper or paint to make tree trunks; use smaller tubes for branches; use tissue papers and a variety of other papers in shades of green and fix to the ceiling; cut bits into strips to hang from the ceiling; birds, animals, insects and fruits can be made in a variety of ways and hung in appropriate places; use finger knitting to make lianas or creepers; make a collection of real rainforest plants such as orchids, rubber plants, African Violet, Christmas Cactus; experiment with how to make the colour *green*.

4   Children could make a study of Brazil to see how important rainforests are to the Brazilians. They will need to use an atlas and the town or school library. Particular emphasis should be placed on the indigenous peoples of the rainforests and the importance of the forest as a home.

5   Ask the children to draw a large tree. Hide in it the things that they know about the rainforest – insects, animals, fruits, people, nuts etc.

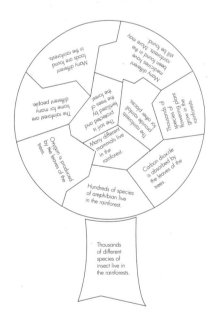

Hazards and Disasters

Name _____

Study the picture below. Match the labels to the hazards and disasters in the picture. Colour in the picture.

earthquake　　　*plague*　　　*volcanic eruption*

typhoon　　　*accident*　　　*fire*　　　*flood*

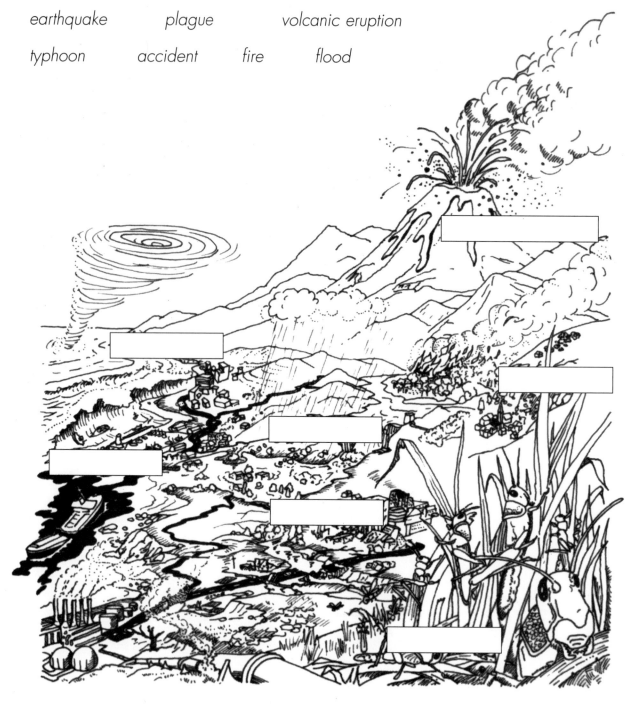

Redrawn with kind permission of Ponce/El Pais

UN Factfile: The United Nations and Disaster Relief

Each year the Earth suffers many natural disasters which can cause death, injury or damage to property. Hazards such as flooding or drought do not always cause disasters but over the last 20 years about 3 million lives have been lost and 1 billion people have lost their homes. Hazards have always existed but disasters are increasing because there are more and more people on the planet and many governments cannot afford to protect their people properly.

The Office of the UN Disaster Relief Coordinator was set up in 1971 by the General Assembly to deal with natural disasters. In 1992, it became part of a new UN Department of Humanitarian Affairs (UNDHA), created to coordinate all types of relief efforts, including relief in 'man-made emergencies'. UNDHA has an emergency supplies warehouse in Pisa, Italy which stores all sorts of necessary items which a country may need when a disaster strikes – motor boats, tool kits, inflatable dinghies, telecommunications units, blankets, tents, plastic water tanks, generators, pick axes, shovels, first aid kits, tool kits and family survival kits.

Workers and supplies may be available from many friendly governments as well as relief organizations. But such help must be coordinated and organized – and that's where the UN comes in – otherwise it can make matters worse. Individuals can also help out by contacting organizations that are providing relief and contributing goods like cans of food or blankets, depending on what is needed. In this way, sometimes people who live far from each other have helped each other.

 Extension activities

1   Ask the children to try to imagine waking up to the terrifying rumbles of an earthquake. They leave the house just before it comes crashing down! Looking around – there are no buildings left standing, no telephones, no water, no electricity, roads ruined and some of their neighbours injured. The only possessions they have are the clothes they are wearing! In groups, ask the children to make a list of all the equipment they might need to survive for at least two weeks.

2   The family survival kits supplied by the UN include many useful items. Ask the children to list the following items in order of importance: soap, disinfectant, iron wire, kitchen utensils, rope, combined shovel/hatchet/saw, stove, 3 multipurpose knife tools, matches, 2 five-litre cans, water purification tablets, a petroleum lamp. Explain why each item might be useful. What else could be included? If disasters happen somewhere would you want to help the people affected? Do you think you would be able to? How?

3   Design a board game with at least 20 squares. The object would be to get from the first square to the last one by rolling dice. But some squares will make players pick up cards. The card can make you move forwards or backwards. Design the cards based on the information here. An example would be: Problem card: Fire: go back 3 squares. The positive cards should make you move forward.

Problem cards	Help cards	Success cards
Fire	UN sends Family Survival kits	Prevention measures work
Flood	Survivors form search parties	People don't panic
Sewage pipes broken	Airport back in action	UN predicted this disaster
Looting	UN coordinates international relief effort	Disaster abates

Motherhood

Name _____

Use the pieces given below to put together a painting by a Chinese artist called Ting Shao Kuang. Work in groups of five. Colour one piece each. Talk to the others in your group to make sure that the colours you are using match up!

UN Factfile: Art and the United Nations

Art is a very important aspect of the United Nations. Individuals and organizations often donate art by famous artists to the UN. The UN has artwork by such world famous artists as Picasso and Chagall. The governments of Member States also donate artwork to the UN. These are often the work of one of their own artists.

The United Nations Postal Administration have their own stamps which can only be used on letters and parcels posted at UN buildings. The World Federation of United Nations Associations (WFUNA) often accompanies the issue of such stamps by commissioning limited edition art prints to go on their first day covers (envelope with stamps postmarked on the first day of issue).

The basis of this worksheet is *Motherhood* which is a painting by Ting Shao Kuang. It forms the cover of the **Primary School Kit on the United Nations**. This was originally a WFUNA first day cover and limited edition art print to accompany the United Nations stamp issue of 4 February 1994 to commemorate the International Year of the Family.

The children should work in groups of five to colour in particular bits of the painting. Remind them that all the pieces will be put together so they must make sure that the colours they choose match with those of the other groups. Hence the activity may take some time. It is an exercise in teamwork, cooperation, leadership and organisation as much as artwork. You may wish to enlarge *Starting Point 16* on to A3 paper.

Extension activities

1   Show the children a full colour version of the painting. In small groups, children could discuss the following questions:
    a   Who are the people in the picture?
    b   What is in the background?
    c   Why has it been painted in these particular colours?
    (Note that a full colour version of this painting appears on the cover of this book.)

2   This painting was originally a first day cover to accompany a United Nations stamp issue. Use one or more of the following techniques to design a stamp for the United Nations on a theme like peace, environment, development, health or education.

    Printing: Children could make a printing block using string, PVA glue and thick, strong card. Lengths of string should be stuck to the piece of card in a pattern of their design. Encourage the children to think about the patterns, the *UN Factfile* and the source painting. Use black ink to print the block. This can be left as a black and white print or, when dry, use drawing inks to fill in the pattern rather like a stained glass window

    Drip painting: This method involves dipping a straw into a pot of black ink. Let the ink drip onto paper and use straws to blow the ink. Once dry, the abstract design can be filled in colours from the picture.

    Pattern: Choose part of the painting to enlarge. Carefully copy the pattern and the colours. Look for patterns in other places such as tiles, fabrics, shells, crockery or animal skins.

    Colour: Using cellophane, children can overlap the colours to see how many new colours can be formed. Each child can choose one colour and collect manufactured and natural objects which are of that colour.

Jitka's Greeting Card

Name _____

Your teacher will tell you the story of Jitka. You can then design and make your own greetings card. Use Jitka's card, the UNICEF logo and the greetings panel which is in seven languages. Which languages are they? Paste them up on to some stiff card and colour in the picture using warm, bright colours. Add features to the faces on Jitka's card.

unicef
United Nations Children's Fund

UN Factfile: United Nations Children's Fund (UNICEF)

In 1945, at the end of the Second World War, there were millions of children who had hardly any food. Many were also without shelter. UNICEF was started in 1946 to care for them. The letters stood for United Nations International Children's Emergency Fund. Today, the letters are still used but the organization is called the United Nations Children's Fund.

The first thing UNICEF did in 1946 was to send milk and blankets to the children of Europe. By 1950 six million children were being helped. By 1953, the emergency work in Europe was finished but many children in Asia, Africa and South America needed help. UNICEF now helps many millions of children in 138 countries all over the world. It has no special funds allocated by the UN. Some of its money is donated on an annual basis by governments and some is given by ordinary people. One of the ways UNICEF raises money is by selling greeting cards. It started like this...

In 1949 a seven-year-old girl called Jitka Samkova painted a brightly coloured picture for UNICEF on a piece of glass. She lived in a village in Czechoslovakia where UNICEF had been helping. In Jitka's class at school children drank UNICEF milk every day. The teacher sent Jitka's picture, with some others as a thank-you present to UNICEF in Prague. From there it went to Vienna where an American lady saw it. She liked it so much that she wrapped it up and took it to New York. The people working for UNICEF in New York decided to make the picture into a Christmas card and sell it. It sold well. The next year, UNICEF made two different Christmas cards, one with the United Nations building in New York on it and the other showing a barge going down a river loaded with supplies. The year after that, several artists gave new designs and each year since then there have been more and more cards – not just Christmas cards but note cards and birthday cards too. All the artists' pictures are still given to the UN.

UNICEF still responds to emergencies but the main thrust of the work is now directed towards long-term goals: primary health care (including immunisation against the six main killer diseases), the provision of clean water and sanitation, nutrition, and the education of children and women. It is estimated that the immunisation programme alone saves three million lives each year. In addition, the community structures set up to deal with immunisation are now being used to meet other goals, such as preventing the spread of AIDS. Mid-nineties goals include saving more babies by promoting breast feeding and by extending the use of Oral Rehydration Salts, eliminating vitamin A deficiency (which causes blindness in children) and achieving universal ratification of the Convention on the Rights of the Child.

Universal Children's Day is the first Monday in October.

Address: UNICEF, 3 United Nations Plaza, Room H-9F, New York, NY 10017, USA.

Extension activities

After telling the children the story about Jitka (see *UN Factfile* above), they can make their card. The languages are: Chinese [vertical], English, French, Spanish, Russian, German and Arabic.

1   Encourage the children to talk about Jitka, her age at the end of the war (1945) and what experiences she might have gone through. Discuss the following questions: a) Why did Jitka paint this particular picture for UNICEF?, b) (This will require an understanding of the Christian Faith.) Was it specially suitable as a Christmas card?

2   Ask the children to send their card to the person who has helped them most during the year.

3   Ask the children to talk about the UNICEF logo. What does it mean to them? Are there any organizations in your area that help children? Find out what they do. Design a logo for them. If they already have a logo, compare your design to theirs. What do the different elements mean to you?

4   UNICEF works for children. Why is this so important? Plan a way of raising money for UNICEF. Organize it with your teacher and some friends. How can children work to help UNICEF?

Where in the World?

Name _____

When a country joins the United Nations, the people of that country sometimes set up a United Nations Association. Over 80 countries have done this so far and they are listed here. Use an atlas to find them on this map. Put the number of the country where you think it is.

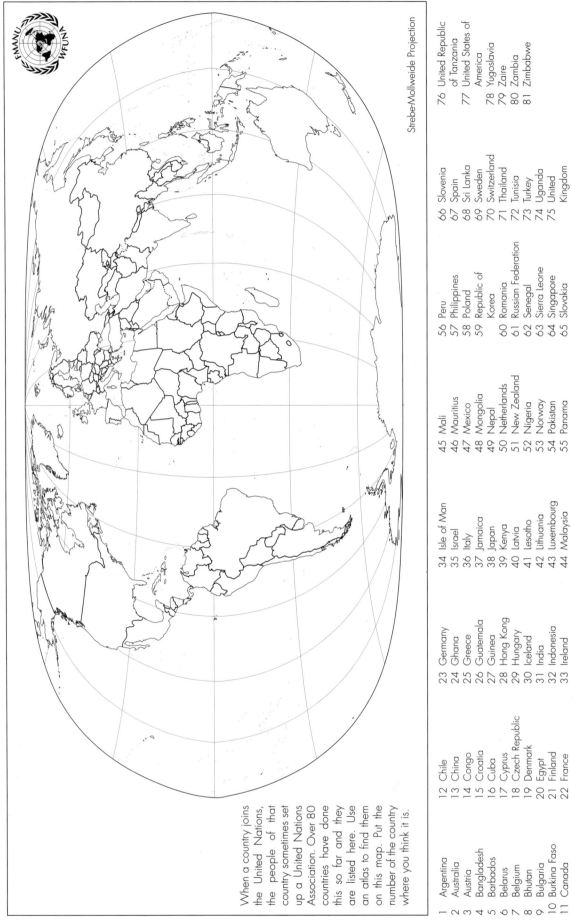

Strebe-Mollweide Projection

1 Argentina
2 Australia
3 Austria
4 Bangladesh
5 Barbados
6 Belarus
7 Belgium
8 Bhutan
9 Bulgaria
10 Burkina Faso
11 Canada

12 Chile
13 China
14 Congo
15 Croatia
16 Cuba
17 Cyprus
18 Czech Republic
19 Denmark
20 Egypt
21 Finland
22 France

23 Germany
24 Ghana
25 Greece
26 Guatemala
27 Guinea
28 Hong Kong
29 Hungary
30 Iceland
31 India
32 Indonesia
33 Ireland

34 Isle of Man
35 Israel
36 Italy
37 Jamaica
38 Japan
39 Kenya
40 Latvia
41 Lesotho
42 Lithuania
43 Luxembourg
44 Malaysia

45 Mali
46 Mauritius
47 Mexico
48 Mongolia
49 Nepal
50 Netherlands
51 New Zealand
52 Nigeria
53 Norway
54 Pakistan
55 Panama

56 Peru
57 Philippines
58 Poland
59 Republic of Korea
60 Romania
61 Russian Federation
62 Senegal
63 Sierra Leone
64 Singapore
65 Slovakia

66 Slovenia
67 Spain
68 Sri Lanka
69 Sweden
70 Switzerland
71 Thailand
72 Tunisia
73 Turkey
74 Uganda
75 United Kingdom

76 United Republic of Tanzania
77 United States of America
78 Yugoslavia
79 Zaire
80 Zambia
81 Zimbabwe

UN Factfile: World Federation of United Nations Associations (WFUNA)

When a country joins the United Nations, the people of that country sometimes set up a United Nations Association. The United Nations is based on the membership of the governments, so United Nations Associations are a way for ordinary citizens to become involved with the UN. They can contact UNAs if they want to find out about the United Nations, or if they have an idea that they would like the United Nations to consider. They may also wish their own government to take a particular course of action at the United Nations.

185 countries were members of the United Nations in March 1995. Of these 81 had set up a United Nations Association. UNAs raise funds and may also recruit members. The World Federation of United Nations Associations (established 2 August 1946) is the organization that all the United Nations Associations can join. One way in which they raise money to help them do their work is by producing first day cover envelopes (envelopes with stamps postmarked on first day of issue) for United Nations stamps. Famous artists from all over the world have given their designs free so that they can be put on to these envelopes.

WFUNA is an international non-governmental organization which devotes itself entirely to the support of the purposes and principles of the United Nations Charter, and to the promotion of public awareness and the understanding of the activities of the United Nations and its agencies.

WFUNA member Associations are established in all parts of the world, in countries of various political, economic and social systems and at different stages of development. It is, however, true to say that, proportionately, there are far fewer in the developing world. WFUNA Headquarters are in Geneva, Switzerland. In addition, WFUNA maintains an office at the UN headquarters in New York as well as regional offices for Africa, Asia and the Pacific.

WFUNA Headquarters postal address:
WFUNA/FMANU,
c/o Palais des Nations,
CH-1211 Geneva 10, Switzerland.

Extension activities

You may wish to photocopy *Starting Point 18* on to A3 paper or use *Resource Point F*.

1   Children could try to name two or more countries that do not have a United Nations Association. Is there a Branch in your town?

2   Children can imagine they are the President of a United Nations Association in their country. They should then think of something they would like the United Nations to do and write a letter to their head of state of foreign minister explaining their idea. Five other people in the class should sign it – this means they will have to explain the idea to others and get them to agree. The letter could be sent in an envelope on which children have drawn something to do with the work of the United Nations such as peace, environment, development, nutrition or health.

3   Children who collect stamps should be encouraged to make a poster showing a set of stamps and where they are from. Children could be asked to produce a stamp design on a piece of card. They should depict United Nation themes. They could then be put together as a collage on the wall.

4   Why do so many poorer countries not have a United Nations Association? Children could be asked to consider this.

Members of the United Nations (March 1995)

Member	Date of admission
Afghanistan	19 Nov 1946
Albania	14 Dec 1955
Algeria	8 Oct 1962
Andorra	28 July 1993
Angola	1 Dec 1976
Antigua and Barbuda	11 Nov 1981
Argentina	24 Oct 1945
Armenia	2 Mar 1992
Australia	1 Nov 1945
Austria	14 Dec 1955
Azerbaijan	2 Mar 1992
Bahamas	18 Sep 1973
Bahrain	21 Sep 1971
Bangladesh	17 Sep 1974
Barbados	9 Dec 1966
Belarus	24 Oct 1945
Belgium	27 Dec 1945
Belize	25 Sep 1981
Benin	20 Sep 1960
Bhutan	21 Sep 1971
Bolivia	14 Nov 1945
Bosnia and Herzegovina	22 May 1992
Botswana	17 Oct 1966
Brazil	24 Oct 1945
Brunei Darussalam	21 Sep 1984
Bulgaria	14 Dec 1955
Burkina Faso	20 Sep 1960
Burundi	18 Sep1962
Cambodia	14 Dec 1955
Cameroon	20 Sep 1960
Canada	9 Nov 1945
Cape Verde	16 Sep 1975
Central African Republic	20 Sep 1960
Chad	20 Sep 1960
Chile	24 Oct 1945
China	24 Oct 1945
Colombia	5 Nov 1945
Comoros	12 Nov 1975
Congo	20 Sep 1960
Costa Rica	2 Nov 1945
Croatia	22 May 1992
Cuba	24 Oct 1945
Cyprus	20 Sep 1960
Czech Republic	19 Jan 1993
Democratic People's Republic of Korea	17 Sep 1991
Denmark	24 Oct 1945
Djibouti	20 Sep 1977
Dominica	18 Dec 1978
Dominican Republic	24 Oct 1945
Ecuador	21 Dec 1945
Egypt	24 Oct 1945
El Salvador	24 Oct 1945
Equatorial Guinea	12 Nov 1968
Eritrea	28 May 1993
Estonia	17 Sep 1991
Ethiopia	13 Nov 1945
Federated States of Micronesia	17 Sep 1991
Fiji	13 Oct 1970
Finland	14 Dec 1955
France	24 Oct 1945
Gabon	20 Sep 1960
Gambia	21 Sep 1965
Georgia	31 Jul 1992
Germany	18 Sep 1973
Ghana	8 Mar 1957
Greece	25 Oct 1945
Grenada	17 Sep 1974
Guatemala	21 Nov 1945
Guinea	12 Dec 1958
Guinea-Bissau	17 Sep 1974
Guyana	20 Sep 1966
Haiti	24 Oct 1945
Honduras	17 Dec 1945
Hungary	14 Dec 1955
Iceland	19 Nov 1946
India	30 Oct 1945
Indonesia	28 Sep 1950
Iran	24 Oct 1945
Iraq	21 Dec 1945
Ireland	14 Dec 1955
Israel	11 May 1949
Italy	14 Dec 1955
Ivory Coast	20 Sep 1960
Jamaica	18 Sep 1962
Japan	18 Dec 1956
Jordan	14 Dec 1955
Kazakhstan	2 Mar 1992
Kenya	16 Dec 1963
Kuwait	14 May 1963
Kyrgyzstan	2 Mar 1992
Lao People's Democratic Republic	14 Dec 1955
Latvia	17 Sep 1991
Lebanon	24 Oct 1945
Lesotho	17 Oct 1966
Liberia	2 Nov 1945
Libya	14 Dec 1955
Liechtenstein	18 Sep 1990
Lithuania	17 Sep 1991
Luxembourg	24 Oct 1945
Madagascar	20 Sep 1960
Malawi	1 Dec 1964
Malaysia	17 Sep 1957
Maldives	21 Sep 1965
Mali	28 Sep 1960
Malta	1 Dec 1964
Marshall Islands	17 Sep 1991
Mauritania	27 Oct 1961
Mauritius	24 Apr 1968
Mexico	7 Nov 1945
Moldova	2 Mar 1992
Monaco	28 May 1993
Mongolia	27 Oct 1961
Morocco	12 Nov 1956
Mozambique	16 Sep 1975
Myanmar	19 Apr 1948
Namibia	23 Apr 1990
Nepal	14 Dec 1955
Netherlands	10 Dec 1945
New Zealand	24 Oct 1945
Nicaragua	24 Oct 1945
Niger	20 Sep 1960
Nigeria	7 Oct 1960
Norway	27 Nov 1945
Oman	7 Oct 1971
Pakistan	30 Sep 1947
Palau	15 Dec 1994
Panama	13 Nov 1945
Papua New Guinea	10 Oct 1975
Paraguay	24 Oct 1945
Peru	31 Oct 1945
Philippines	24 Oct 1945
Poland	24 Oct 1945
Portugal	14 Dec 1955
Qatar	21 Sep 1971
Republic of Korea	17 Sep 1991
Romania	14 Dec 1955
Russian Federation	24 Oct 1945
Rwanda	18 Sep 1962
Saint Kitts and Nevis	23 Sep 1983
Saint Lucia	18 Sep 1979
Saint Vincent and the Grenadines	16 Sep 1980
Samoa	15 Dec 1976
San Marino	2 Mar 1992
Sao Tome and Principe	16 Sep 1975
Saudi Arabia	24 Oct 1945
Senegal	28 Sep 1960
Seychelles	21 Sep 1976
Sierra Leone	27 Sep 1961
Singapore	21 Sep 1965
Slovak Republic	19 Jan 1993
Slovenia	22 May 1992
Solomon Islands	19 Sep 1978
Somalia	20 Sep 1960
South Africa	7 Nov 1945
Spain	14 Dec 1955
Sri Lanka	14 Dec 1955
Sudan	12 Nov 1956
Suriname	4 Dec 1975
Swaziland	24 Sep 1968
Sweden	19 Nov 1946
Syria	24 Oct 1945
Tajikistan	2 Mar 1992
Thailand	16 Dec 1946
The Former Yugoslav Republic of Macedonia	8 April 1993
Togo	20 Sep 1960
Trinidad and Tobago	18 Sep 1962
Tunisia	12 Nov 1956
Turkey	24 Oct 1945
Turkmenistan	2 Mar 1992
Uganda	25 Oct 1962
Ukraine	24 Oct 1945
United Arab Emirates	9 Dec 1971
United Kingdom	24 Oct 1945
United Republic of Tanzania	14 Dec 1961
United States of America	24 Oct 1945
Uruguay	18 Dec 1945
Uzbekistan	2 Mar 1992
Vanuatu	15 Sep 1981
Venezuela	15 Nov 1945
Vietnam	20 Sep 1977
Yemen	30 Sep 1947
Yugoslavia (Serbia/ Montenegro)	24 Oct 1945
Zaire	20 Sep 1960
Zambia	1 Dec 1964
Zimbabwe	25 Aug 1980
Total	185 members

United Nation Days and Years

A calendar for action

Decades

1985-1994	Transport and Communications Decade for Asia and the Pacific
1988-1997	World Decade for Cultural Development
1990-2000	International Decade for the Eradication of Colonialism
1990-2000	UN Decade of International Law
1990-2000	Third Disarmament Decade
1990-2000	Second Industrial Development Decade for Africa
1990-2000	International Decade for Natural Disaster Reduction
1991-2000	Second Transport and Communications Decade in Africa
1991-2000	Fourth United Nations Development Decade
1991-2000	UN Decade Against Drug Abuse
1995-2005	UN Decade for Human Rights Education

April 7
World Health Day

Years

1992	International Space Year
1993	International Year for the World's Indigenous Peoples
1994	International Year of the Family
	International Year of Sports and the Olympic Ideal
1995	50th Anniversary of the United Nations
	International Year for Tolerance
	Fourth World Conference on Women
	World Summit for Social Development
1996	International Year for the Eradication of Poverty
1999	International Year of the Elderly

June 5
World Environment Day

Weeks and Days

8 March	International Women's Day
21 March	International Day for the Elimination of Racial Discrimination
22 March	World Day for Water
23 March	World Meteorological Day
7 April	World Health Day
3 May	World Press Freedom Day
15 May	International Day of Families
17 May	World Telecommunications Day
31 May	World No-Tobacco Day
4 June	International Day of Innocent Children Victims of Aggression
5 June	World Environment Day
26 June	International Day Against Drug Abuse and Illicit Trafficking
11 July	World Population Day
8 September	International Literacy Day
3rd Tuesday in September	International Day of Peace: Opening of UN General Assembly
September	World Maritime Day (during last week of month)
1 October	International Day for the Elderly
1st Monday in October	World Habitat Day
	Universal Children's Day
9 October	World Post Day
13 October	International Day for Natural Disaster Reduction
16 October	World Food Day
24 October	UN Day
	World Development Information Day
24-30 October	Week for Disarmament and Development
9-14 November	International Week of Science and Peace
20 November	Africa Industrialization Day
29 November	International Day of Solidarity with the Palestinian People
1 December	World AIDS Day
3 December	International Day of Disabled Persons
5 December	International Volunteer Day for Economic and Social Development
10 December	Human Rights Day

October 24
United Nations Day

The United Nations System

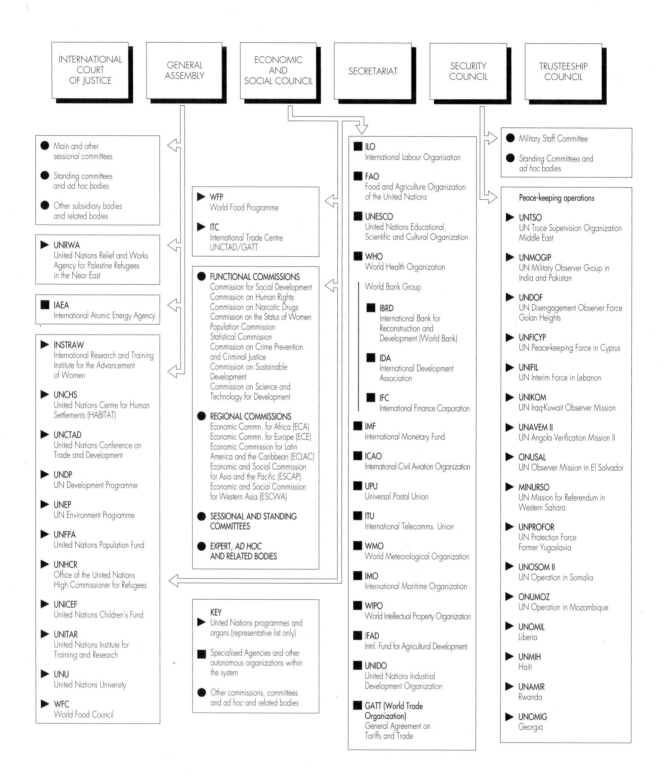

| INTERNATIONAL COURT OF JUSTICE | GENERAL ASSEMBLY | ECONOMIC AND SOCIAL COUNCIL | SECRETARIAT | SECURITY COUNCIL | TRUSTEESHIP COUNCIL |

GENERAL ASSEMBLY bodies:

● Main and other sessional committees

● Standing committees and *ad hoc* bodies

● Other subsidiary bodies and related bodies

▶ UNRWA
United Nations Relief and Works Agency for Palestine Refugees in the Near East

■ IAEA
International Atomic Energy Agency

▶ INSTRAW
International Research and Training Institute for the Advancement of Women

▶ UNCHS
United Nations Centre for Human Settlements (HABITAT)

▶ UNCTAD
United Nations Conference on Trade and Development

▶ UNDP
UN Development Programme

▶ UNEP
UN Environment Programme

▶ UNFPA
United Nations Population Fund

▶ UNHCR
Office of the United Nations High Commissioner for Refugees

▶ UNICEF
United Nations Children's Fund

▶ UNITAR
United Nations Institute for Training and Research

▶ UNU
United Nations University

▶ WFC
World Food Council

ECONOMIC AND SOCIAL COUNCIL bodies:

▶ WFP
World Food Programme

▶ ITC
International Trade Centre UNCTAD/GATT

● FUNCTIONAL COMMISSIONS
Commission for Social Development
Commission on Human Rights
Commission on Narcotic Drugs
Commission on the Status of Women
Population Commission
Statistical Commission
Commission on Crime Prevention and Criminal Justice
Commission on Sustainable Development
Commission on Science and Technology for Development

● REGIONAL COMMISSIONS
Economic Commn. for Africa (ECA)
Economic Commn. for Europe (ECE)
Economic Commission for Latin America and the Caribbean (ECLAC)
Economic and Social Commission for Asia and the Pacific (ESCAP)
Economic and Social Commission for Western Asia (ESCWA)

● SESSIONAL AND STANDING COMMITTEES

● EXPERT, *AD HOC* AND RELATED BODIES

KEY

▶ United Nations programmes and organs (representative list only)

■ Specialised Agencies and other autonomous organizations within the system

● Other commissions, committees and *ad hoc* and related bodies

SECRETARIAT bodies:

■ ILO
International Labour Organisation

■ FAO
Food and Agriculture Organization of the United Nations

■ UNESCO
United Nations Educational, Scientific and Cultural Organization

■ WHO
World Health Organization

World Bank Group

■ IBRD
International Bank for Reconstruction and Development (World Bank)

■ IDA
International Development Association

■ IFC
International Finance Corporation

■ IMF
International Monetary Fund

■ ICAO
International Civil Aviation Organization

■ UPU
Universal Postal Union

■ ITU
International Telecomms. Union

■ WMO
World Meteorological Organization

■ IMO
International Maritime Organization

■ WIPO
World Intellectual Property Organization

■ IFAD
Intnl. Fund for Agricultural Development

■ UNIDO
United Nations Industrial Development Organization

■ GATT (World Trade Organization)
General Agreement on Tariffs and Trade

SECURITY COUNCIL bodies:

● Military Staff Committee

● Standing Committees and *ad hoc* bodies

Peace-keeping operations

▶ UNTSO
UN Truce Supervision Organization Middle East

▶ UNMOGIP
UN Military Observer Group in India and Pakistan

▶ UNDOF
UN Disengagement Observer Force Golan Heights

▶ UNFICYP
UN Peace-keeping Force in Cyprus

▶ UNIFIL
UN Interim Force in Lebanon

▶ UNIKOM
UN Iraq-Kuwait Observer Mission

▶ UNAVEM II
UN Angola Verification Mission II

▶ ONUSAL
UN Observer Mission in El Salvador

▶ MINURSO
UN Mission for Referendum in Western Sahara

▶ UNPROFOR
UN Protection Force Former Yugoslavia

▶ UNOSOM II
UN Operation in Somalia

▶ ONUMOZ
UN Operation in Mozambique

▶ UNOMIL
Liberia

▶ UNMIH
Haiti

▶ UNAMIR
Rwanda

▶ UNOMIG
Georgia

The main organs of the United Nations

General Assembly: The General Assembly is composed of representatives of nearly all the nations of the world. It is where countries can voice their concerns to the rest of the world. By March 1995 the total membership had reached 185 nations. Switzerland is one country which is not a member of the UN, although the European headquarters of the UN are in Geneva. Each Member State has a single vote no matter what its size or wealth. The General Assembly normally meets in New York. Each country is represented by a senior diplomat but, at times, foreign ministers or even heads of state attend meetings of the General Assembly. It meets regularly from September to mid-December and also holds special sessions when the need arises. The General Assembly serves as a forum where Member States may discuss any matters of global concern. It promotes the cooperation of nations in social and economic affairs and encourages the observation of human rights for all. It has special committees on such matters as disarmament, finance, humanitarian issues, and social and economic concerns. Deliberations in the General Assembly have resulted in significant agreements and the creation of new international law. These agreements, or adopted resolutions, are only recommendations and, as such, cannot be enforced. However, they carry great weight because they represent the opinion of a majority of countries.

Security Council: The main function of the Security Council is to maintain international peace. The Security Council meets whenever necessary in New York. It has 15 members, five of which are permanent. They are China, France, the Russian Federation, the United Kingdom and the United States. The other 10 members are elected by the General Assembly, on the basis of geographic representation, for two-year terms, five being selected each year. Under the terms of the Charter, all the members of the UN have agreed to accept the decisions of the Security Council.

While the other organs of the UN, such as the General Assembly, can only make recommendations to governments, the Security Council has the power to take decisions which Member States are obliged to carry out. However, any one of the five permanent members can forbid an action even if the other 14 are in favour — this is called veto power. The Security Council has not always been successful. But its success is only dependent on the will of governments to carry out its resolutions.

Economic and Social Council: ECOSOC, as it is often called, deals with the matters which many of our Ministries deal with. The Council has 54 members who serve for three years — 18 new members are elected each year. Voting is by a simple majority. It holds one month-long session each year. It discusses, studies and makes recommendations to the General Assembly relating to economic development, environmental issues, human rights and other economic issues. It also coordinates the work of the Commissions and the Specialized Agencies such as the World Health Organization (WHO), the International Labour Organisation (ILO), the Food and Agriculture Organization (FAO) and the UN Educational, Scientific and Cultural Organization (UNESCO).

The International Court of Justice: The Court consists of 15 judges elected by the General Assembly. The judges are chosen on the basis of their qualifications and not on their nationality. However, no two judges can be from the same country. The seat of the Court is in The Hague, Netherlands. Member States can refer matters to it such as border disputes, fishing and mineral rights and other matters to do with the Charter. The General Assembly or the Security Council may ask the Court for an advisory opinion on any matter.

Trusteeship Council: This Council supervised the administration Trust Territories — former colonies placed under the trusteeship system as a means of ensuring that states responsible for them promoted their progress towards self-determination. The last of the eleven such Trust Territories, Palau (one of Micronesian groups of islands), achieved independence in November 1994, and became the UN's newest Member State the following month. The Council has since formally suspended its operation.

The Secretariat: The Secretariat is the 'civil service' of the UN. It has an international staff of 15 000 to service the various commissions and agencies. The Headquarters are in New York. Other UN centres are in Geneva and Vienna. The head of the Secretariat is the Secretary-General.

What has the United Nations done?

With the help of other organizations and governments, the UN has played a key role in the following global achievements…

Human Rights and International Standards

- strengthened and expanded the body of international law through over 300 treaties
- set standards for human rights based on the Universal Declaration of Human Rights
- supported democracy by assisting elections in over 45 countries
- provided technical assistance on electoral matters in over 30 countries
- promoted self-determination with over 80 Member States achieving independence since 1945
- provided international protection and assistance to more than 30 million refugees since 1951 (currently UNHCR helps 20 million refugees, mostly women and children)
- helped millions of Palestinian refugees by providing free schooling, health care and assistance (currently UNRWA supports 2.75 million refugees in the Near East)
- encouraged the free flow of information through UNESCO
- promoted a greater recognition of women's rights through INSTRAW and UNIFEM
- highlighted minority issues including those to do with the disabled and indigenous peoples
- promoted children's rights through the Convention on the Rights of the Child
- ensured that mail and broadcast systems operate as intended thanks to the UPU and ITU
- made travel by sea safer through IMO
- introduced a system of universal aeronautical meteorological codes through WMO
- set standards for air traffic through ICAO
- preserved and protected the world's cultural heritage at 440 sites in 100 countries through UNESCO
- linked scientists, promoted research and strengthened numerous university departments
- led the international effort to eradicate illiteracy especially amongst girls and women
- established standards for water quality, pharmaceuticals, food safety and chemicals through WHO
- helped reduce the toll of work-related accidents through standards established by ILO
- established and monitored nuclear safety standards and peaceful uses of atomic energy through IAEA

Conflict Prevention and Resolution

- established 35 peace-keeping operations to help find solutions to conflicts through negotiations
- undertaken peace-making in troubled areas such as in Afghanistan, El Salvador and the Iran-Iraq war
- fought apartheid through, for example, an arms embargo imposed by the Security Council
- pioneered 'children as a zone of peace' to support children in conflict zones
- promoted disarmament through treaties developed by the Conference on Disarmament

Sustainable Development

- battled poverty and promoted sustainable development in over 170 countries through UNDP
- strengthened industrial development in the developing countries through UNIDO
- helped focus economic policy on human need
- helped remove trade barriers through GATT
- helped expand exports and improve imports through UNCTAD
- promoted international trade and technology transfer through WIPO which has a register of 280 000 international trademarks
- linked community groups with aid projects through UNESCO Co-Action
- acted as an early warning system on the state of the Earth's atmosphere through WMO
- led the international effort to preserve and protect the environment through UNEP and UNESCO
- combatted drug abuse and trafficking through international conventions and helped farmers find alternative sources of income
- enabled reductions in population growth, infant mortality and fertility rates through UNFPA
- improved women's literacy in the developing world from 36% in 1970 to 55% in 1990
- improved food production for the poorest in over 100 countries through IFAD
- co-ordinated disaster relief and rehabilitation through UNDRO
- improved agricultural techniques through FAO
- limited deforestation and promoted sustainable forestry through FAO and UNDP
- monitored world fisheries through FAO

Health

- eradicated smallpox in 1980 after a 13 year campaign at a cost equal to 3 hours of world arms expenditure (WHO)
- eradicated poliomyelitis from the Western hemisphere and aims for global eradication by 2000
- immunised 80% of the world's children against polio, tetanus, measles, whooping cough, diphtheria and TB (UNICEF)
- saved more than 7 million children from going blind as a result of river blindness (WHO)
- cut child death rates in developing countries by half since 1960 (UNICEF, UNFPA, WHO and others)
- led the world fight against AIDS through WHO
- provided aid and prevented starvation by distributing 2 million tons of food each year (WFP)

The Preamble to the United Nations Charter

'We the peoples of the United Nations determined to save succeeding generations from the scourge of war, which twice in our lifetime has brought untold sorrow to mankind, and to reaffirm faith in fundamental human rights, in the dignity and worth of the human person, in the equal rights of men and women and of nations large and small, and to establish conditions under which justice and respect for the obligations arising from treaties and other sources of international law can be maintained, and to promote social progress and better standards of life in larger freedom, and for these ends, to practice tolerance and live together in peace with one another as good neighbours, and to unite our strength to maintain international peace and security, and to ensure, by the acceptance of principles and the institution of methods, that armed force shall not be used, save in the common interest, and to employ international machinery for the promotion of the economic and social advancement of all peoples, have resolved to combine our efforts to accomplish these aims.

Accordingly, our respective Governments, through representatives assembled in the city of San Francisco, who have exhibited their full powers found to be in good and due form, have agreed to the present Charter of the United Nations and do hereby establish an international organization to be known as the United Nations.'

26 June 1945

The full text of the Charter is available from the UN's Department of Public Information and is also printed in *Everyone's United Nations* (see *Resource Point L*)

World Map

Strebe-Mollweide Projection

A summary of

the United Nations Convention on the Rights of the Child

- Children have the right to be with their family or those who will care for them best

- Children have the right to enough food and clean water

- Children have the right to an adequate standard of living

- Children have the right to health care

- Disabled children have the right to special care and training

- Children must be allowed to speak their own language and practise their own religion and culture

- Children have the right to play

- Children have the right to free education

- Children have the right to be kept safe and not be hurt, exploited or neglected

- Children must not be used as cheap labour or soldiers

- Children have the right to protection from cruelty, neglect and injustice

- Children have the right to express their own opinions and to meet together to express their views

United Nations Logos

(United Nations)

(United Nations Educational,
Scientific and Cultural Organization)

(United Nations Centre for Human
Rights)

(Universal Postal Union)

(United Nations Children's Fund)

(World Intellectual Property
Organization)

(Office of the United Nations High
Commissioner for Refugees)

(World Health Organization)

(United Nations Environment
Programme)

(United Nations International Civil
Aviation Organization)

(United Nations International Research and Training
Institute for the Advancement of Women)

United Nations Logos

(Food and Agriculture Organization
of the United Nations)

(United Nations Development
Programme)

(International Fund for Agricultural
Development)

(International Labour Organisation)

(International Telecommunications
Union)

(International Maritime Organization)

(International Monetary Fund)

(World Meteorological Organization)

(World Bank)

(United Nations Centre for Human
Settlements) (HABITAT)

(International Atomic Energy Agency)

(UN University)

A Paper Crane

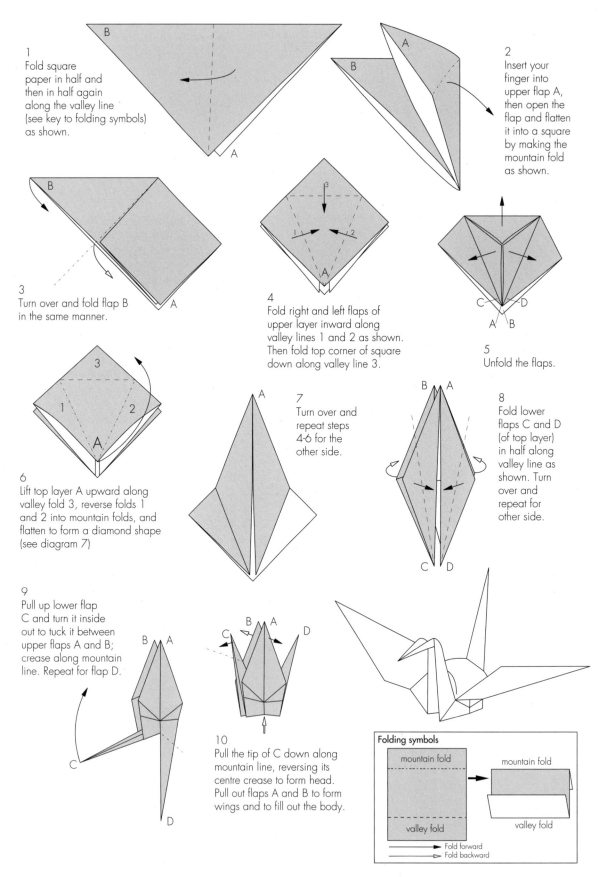

1
Fold square paper in half and then in half again along the valley line (see key to folding symbols) as shown.

2
Insert your finger into upper flap A, then open the flap and flatten it into a square by making the mountain fold as shown.

3
Turn over and fold flap B in the same manner.

4
Fold right and left flaps of upper layer inward along valley lines 1 and 2 as shown. Then fold top corner of square down along valley line 3.

5
Unfold the flaps.

6
Lift top layer A upward along valley fold 3, reverse folds 1 and 2 into mountain folds, and flatten to form a diamond shape (see diagram 7)

7
Turn over and repeat steps 4-6 for the other side.

8
Fold lower flaps C and D (of top layer) in half along valley line as shown. Turn over and repeat for other side.

9
Pull up lower flap C and turn it inside out to tuck it between upper flaps A and B; crease along mountain line. Repeat for flap D.

10
Pull the tip of C down along mountain line, reversing its centre crease to form head. Pull out flaps A and B to form wings and to fill out the body.

Folding symbols

mountain fold	mountain fold
valley fold	valley fold

→ Fold forward
⇢ Fold backward

A Paper Dove

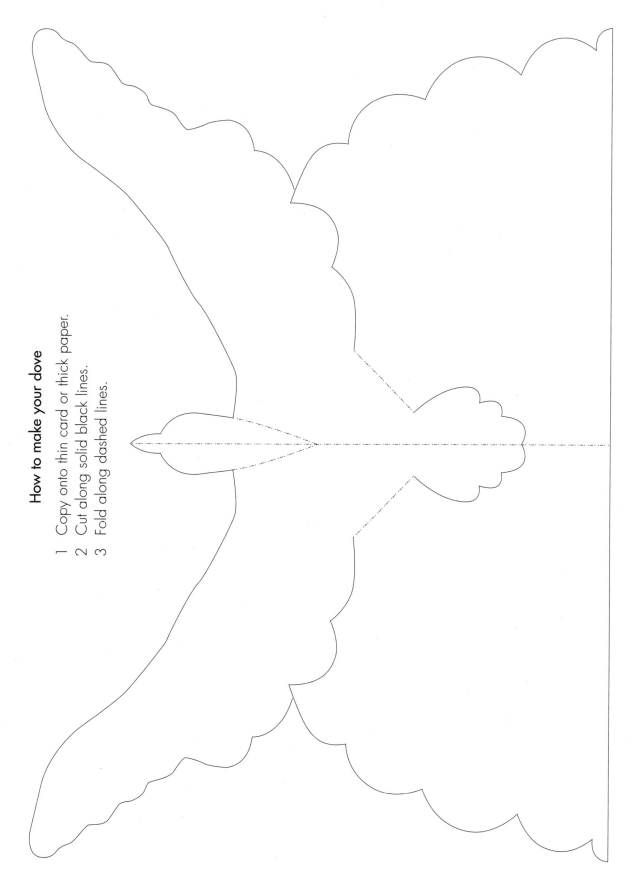

How to make your dove

1 Copy onto thin card or thick paper.
2 Cut along solid black lines.
3 Fold along dashed lines.

Getting Information on the United Nations 1

The United Nations Information Centres

The purpose of this network can be found in a 1946 resolution of the General Assembly: *"The United Nations cannot achieve its purposes unless the peoples of the world are fully informed of its aims and activities."*

The Information Centres, or UNIC's, provide a variety of services. These include promoting information on the activities of the United Nations and the Specialised Agencies and maintaining an up-to-date collection of all United Nations documents and other official publications. They assist representatives of the media, maintain relations with government and major non-governmental organizations concerning United Nations activities and seek the support of other organizations for these activities. They also perform a variety of administrative tasks on behalf of various organizations of the United Nations System.

The centres receive daily from New York an electronic transmission providing the latest information from around the world on United Nations activities. They are thus able to provide the media, researchers and others with details of these developments. They respond daily to a large volume of requests for information about the UN received by telephone, mail, facsimile and personal visits. They produce weekly newsletters and issue press releases.

They often provide a library service and maintain a collection of films and videos, photographs and slides relating to UN activities. Your enquiries should be by letter and addressed to a specific query. (See *Resource Point M.*)

ACCRA, PO Box 2339, Accra, Ghana (233-21) 665-511/666-851-5
ADDIS ABABA, PO Box 3001, Addis Ababa, Ethiopia (251-1) 510-172
ALGIERS, Boîte Postale 823, Alger-Gare, Algeria (213-2) 744-902/744-903
AMMAN, PO Box 927115, Amman, Jordan (9626) 69 4351 (A) - 606847 (B)
ANKARA, P.K. 407, Ankara, Turkey (90-4) 426-5485
ANTANANARIVO, Boîte Postale 1348, Antananarivo, Madagascar, 241-15
ASUNCION, Casilla de Correo 1107, Asunción, Paraguay (595-21) 493025/493026/493027
ATHENS, GR-10558 Athens, Greece (30-1) 523-0640
BANGKOK, Bangkok 10200, Thailand (66-2) 282-9607
BEIRUT, PO Box 4656, Beirut, Lebanon (962-6) 867 700/800 002
BRAZZAVILLE, PO Box 13210/or 1018, Brazzaville, Congo (242) 83-50-90/83-58-48
BRUSSELS, Avenue de Broqueville 40, 1200 Brussels (32-2) 770-5047
BUCHAREST, PO Box 1-701, Bucharest, Romania (40-1) 211-32-42
BUENOS AIRES, Junín 1940, 1 piso, 1113 Beunos Aires, Argentina (54-1) 801-0155
BUJUMBURA, Boîte Postale 2160, Bujumbura, Burundi (257) 225-018
CAIRO, Boite Postale 262, Cairo, Egypt (20-2) 769-595
COLOMBO, PO Box 1505, Colombo, Sri Lanka (94-1) 580-691
COPENHAGEN, 37 HC Andersens Boulevard, DK-1553 Copenhagen V, Denmark (45) 33-12-21-20
DAKAR, Boite Postale 154, Dakar, Sénégal (221) 233-070, 234-066
DAR-ES-SALAAM, PO Box 9224, Dar-es-Salaam, United Republic of Tanzania (255-51) 46278
DHAKA, GPO Box 3658, Dhaka 1000, Bangladesh (880-2) 817898/817868/326434
GENEVA, Palais des Nations, 1211 Geneva 10, Switzerland (41-22) 917 2300/917 2325/917 2324
HARARE, PO Box 4408, Harare, Zimbabwe (263-4) 79-15-21/70-46-79
ISLAMABAD, PO Box 1107, Islamabad, Pakistan (92-51) 210-610/213-465/213-553
JAKARTA, Gedung Dewan Pers, Fifth Floor, 32-34 Jalan Kebon Sirih, Jakarta, Indonesia (62-21) 380-0292/378050
KABUL, PO Box 5, Kabul, Afghanistan 24437/22684
KATHMANDU, PO Box 107, Pulchowk, Kathmandu, Nepal (977-1) 524366
KHARTOUM, PO Box 1992, Khartoum, Republic of the Sudan 77816/73772
KINSHASA, Boite Postale 7248, Kinshasa, Republic of Zaire (243-12) 30-400 Ext 67

LAGOS, PO Box 1068, Lagos, Nigeria (234-1) 2694886

LA PAZ, Apartado Postal 9072, La Paz, Bolivia (591-2) 358-590/358-591

LIMA, PO BOx 14-0199, Lima, Peru (51-14) 40-6145/41-8745/22-0879

LISBON, Rua Latino Coelho, 1, Ed Aviz, Bloco A-1, 10°, 1000 Lisbon, Portugal (351-1) 352-9232

LOME, Boite Postale 911, Lomé, Togo (228) 212-306

LONDON, 18 Buckingham Gate, London SW1E 6LB (44-71) 630-1981-1987

LUSAKA, PO Box 32905, Lusaka 10101, Republic of Zambia (260-1) 228-487/228-488

MADRID, PO Box 3400, 28080 Madrid, Spain (34-1) 555-8087/555-8142

MANAGUA, Reporto Bolonia, Porton Hospital Militar, IC Lago, Managua, Nicaragua (505-2) 660-507/661-701

MANAMA, PO Box 26004, Manama, Bahrain (973) 231-046

MANILA, PO Box 7285 (DAPO), 1300 Domestic Road, Pasay City, Metro Manila, Philippines (63-2) 892-0611

MASERU, PO Box 301, Maseru 100, Lesotho (266) 312 496

MEXICO CITY, Presidente Masaryk 29-7°, piso, 11570 Mexico, D.F. (52-5) 250-1364

MOSCOW, 4/16 Ulitsa Lunacharskogo, Moscow 121002, Russian Federation (7-095) 241-2894

NAIROBI, PO Box 34135, Nairobi, Kenya (254-2) 623292/3, 623798, 622545

NEW DELHI, 55 Lodi Estate, New Delhi-110003, India (91-11) 462 34 39

OUAGADOUGOU, Boite Postale 135, Ouagadougou 01, Burkina Faso (226) 30-60-76

PANAMA CITY, PO Box 6-9083 El Dorado, Panamá, Republic of Panamá (507) 232-198

PARIS, 1 rue Miollia, 75732, Paris Cedex 15, France (33-1) 45-68-49-00

PORT OF SPAIN, PO Box 130, Port-of-Spain, Trinidad (1-809) 623-4813

PRAGUE, Panska 5, 11000 Prague 1, Czech Republic (42-2) 24-21-10-49

RABAT, Boite Postale 601, Rabat, Morocco (212-77) 686-33/632-04

RIO DE JANEIRO, Palácio Itamaraty, Av. Marechal Floriano 196, 20080 Rio de Janeiro (55-21) 253-2211

ROME, Palazzetto Venezia, Piazza San Marco 50, 00186 Rome, Italy (39-6) 678-9907

SANA'A, PO Box 551, Sana'a, Republic of Yemen (967-1) 215-505/8

SAN SALVADOR, Apartado Postal 2157, San Salvador, El Salvador (503) 23-4466

SANTA FE DE BOGOTA, Apartado Aéeo 058964, Santa Fé de Bogotá 2, Colombia (57-1) 257-6044

SANTIAGO, Comisión Económica para América, Latinay el Caribe, Avda, Dag Hammarskjôld s/n, Casilla 179D, Santiago, Chile (56-2) 210-2000, 228-1947

SYDNEY, PO Box 4045, Sydney NSW 2001, Australia (61-2) 283-1144

TEHERAN, PO Box 15875-4557, Teheran, Islamic Republic of Iran (98-21) 886 2812 to 5

TOKYO, UNU Building, 8th Floor, 53-70, Jingumac 5-chome, Shibuya-ku, Tokyo 150, Japan (81-3) 5467 4455

TRIPOLI, PO Box 286, Tripoli, Libyan Arab, Jamahiriya (218-21) 77885; 70251

TUNIS, Boite Postale 863, Tunis, Tunisia (216-1) 560-203

VIENNA, PO Box 500, A-1400 Vienna, Austria (43-1) 211-31-4666

WASHINGTON DC, 1775 K Street, N.W. Suite 400, Washington, DC 20006, USA (202) 331 8670

WINDHOEK, Private Bag 13351, Windhoek, Namibia (264) 61-233034

YANGON, PO Box 230, Yangon, Myanmar (95-01) 92911

YAOUNDE, Boite Postale 836, Yaoundé, Republic of Cameroon (237) 22-50-43

Getting Information on the United Nations 2

United Nations

United Nations Headquarters
New York, NY 10017
USA
Tel (1) (212) 963 1234

United Nations Office at Geneva
Palais des Nations
CH-1211 Geneva 10
Switzerland
Tel (41) (22) 907 1234

United Nations Office at Vienna
Vienna International Centre
PO Box 500
A-1400 Vienna
Austria
Tel (43) (1) 211 31
            + extension (0 for switchboard)

United Nations Children's Fund (UNICEF)
3 United Nations Plaza
Room H-9F
New York NY 10017
USA
Tel (1) (212) 326 7000

United Nations Conference on Trade and Development (UNCTAD)
Palais des Nations
CH-1211 Geneva 10
Switzerland
Tel (41) (22) 730 0111

United Nations Development Programme (UNDP)
1 United Nations Plaza
New York NY 10017
USA
Tel (1) (212) 906 5000

United Nations Environment Programme (UNEP)
PO Box 30552
Nairobi
Kenya
Tel (254) (2) 333930

United Nations Population Fund (UNFPA)
220 East 42nd Street
New York NY 10017
USA
Tel (1) (212) 850 5631

United Nations Institute for Training and Research (UNITAR)
Palais des Nations
CH-1211 Geneva 10
Switzerland
Tel (41) (22) 798 5850

United Nations Relief and Works Agency for Palestinian Refugees in the Near East (UNRWA)
Vienna International Centre
PO Box 700
A-1400 Vienna
Austria
Tel (43) (1) 211 31 + extension

United Nations University (UNU)
Toho Seimei Building
15-1, Shibuya 2-chome
Shibuya-ku
Tokyo 150
Japan
Tel (81) (3) 499 2811

United Nations Centre for Human Settlements (HABITAT)
Room M-337
PO Box 30030
Nairobi
Kenya
Tel (254) (2) 333930/520600

Office of the United Nations High Commissioner for Refugees (UNHCR)
Case Postale 2500,
CH-1211, Geneva 2 Dépôt
Switzerland
Tel (41) (22) 739 8111

World Food Council (WFC)
Via delle Terme di Caracalla
1-00100 Rome
Italy
Tel (39) (6) 52251

International Court of Justice (ICJ)
Peace Palace
2517 KJ The Hague
The Netherlands
Tel (31) (70) 392 4441

International Research and Training Institute for the Advancement of Women (INSTRAW)
Calle Cesar Nicolas Penson 102-A
Santo Domingo
Dominican Republic
Tel (500) (809) 685 2111/7

International Trade Centre UNCTAD/GATT (ITC)
Palais des Nations
1211 Geneva 10
Switzerland
Tel (41) (22) 917 1234

World Food Programme (WFP)
426 Via Cristoforo Colombo
00145 Rome
Italy
Tel (39) (6) 52251

Specialised Agencies and Related Organizations

International Labour Organisation (ILO)
4 route des Morillons
CH-1211 Geneva 22
Switzerland
Tel (41) (22) 799 6111

Food and Agriculture Organization of the United Nations (FAO)
Via delle Terme di Caracalla
1-00100 Rome
Italy
Tel (39) (6) 52251

United Nations Educational, Scientific and Cultural Organization (UNESCO)
F-75352 Paris 07SP
France
Tel (33) (1) 45681000

International Civil Aviation Organization (ICAO)
1000 Sherbrooke Street West
Suite 327
Montreal, PQ
H3A 2R2 Canada
Tel (1) (514) 285 8219

World Health Organization (WHO)
20 Avenue Appia
CH-1211 Geneva 27
Switzerland
Tel (41) (22) 791 2111

World Bank/International Finance Corporation (IFC)
1818 H Street, NW
Washington DC 20433
USA
Tel (1) (202) 477 1234

International Monetary Fund (IMF)
700 19th Street, NW
Washington DC 20431
USA
Tel (1) (202) 623 7000

Universal Postal Union (UPU)
Weltpoststrasse 4
3000 Berne 15
Switzerland
Tel (41) (31) 350 3111

International Telecommunication Union
(ITU)
Place des Nations
Room 306A
CH-1211 Geneva 20
Switzerland
Tel (41) (22) 730 5111

World Meteorological Organization
(WMO)
41 avenue Giuseppe-Motta
Geneva
Switzerland
Tel (41) (22) 730 8111

International Maritime Organization
(IMO)
4 Albert Embankment
London
SE1 7SR
United Kingdom
Tel (44) (171) 735 7611

World Intellectual Property Organization
(WIPO)
34 chemin des Colombettes
CH-1211 Geneva 20
Switzerland
Tel (41) (22) 730 9111

International Fund for Agricultural
Development (IFAD)
107 Via del Serafico
Room 408
00142 Rome
Italy
Tel (39) (6) 54591

United Nations Industrial Development
Organization (UNIDO)
Vienna International Centre
PO Box 300
A-1400 Vienna
Austria
Tel (43) (1) 21131+ extension

International Atomic Energy Agency
(IAEA)
Vienna International Centre
PO Box 100
A-1400 Vienna
Austria
Tel (43) (1) 2360 + extension

General Agreement on Tariffs and Trade
(GATT)
Centre William Rappard
154 rue de Lausanne
CH-1211 Geneva 21
Switzerland
Tel (41) (22) 739 5111

Resources for teaching about the United Nations

The materials contained in this resource list are not exhaustive. They have been chosen because they address directly the United Nations and will assist classroom teachers if they wish to prepare themselves prior to using the *Kits on the United Nations*. You can order the resources through local distributors or, in case of UN publications, by writing directly to UN Publications (2 United Nations Plaza, Room DC2-853, Dept. 007C, New York, NY 10017, Fax (212) 963-3489). UN Information Centres in your country should also be able to help you with information, especially regarding videos (See *Resource Point K*).

General

A Life in Peace and War, Brian Urquhart, Harper and Row, UK (1987)
A Question of Refugees, Carol Barker, Macdonald, UK (1988)
An Instructional Guide to Teaching About the United Nations, UNA-USA, 1993
Children of the World – Learning Together at the United Nations, Martin Meyer, Madison Books (1990)
Creating a Sustainable World (for students in grades 7-12), UNA-USA, 1993
Educating for Peace Project, UNA-USA, 1993
Forty Years of the United Nations, US Bajpai, Lancer, India (1990)
Geography Teaching and the UN, David Barrs in International Understanding Through Geography, Ed. Speak and Wiegand, Geographical Association, UK (1993)
Rescue Mission: Planet Earth, Peace Child International, Kingfisher, UK, 1994
United Nations – Its Work in the World, Carol Barker, Macdonald, UK (1986)
We the Young People – A children's history of the United Nations written by young people, Peace Child International, Buntingford, UK (due out 1995)

United Nations publications

A World for Everybody, UNESCO (1979)
An Agenda for Peace, UN Publications (1995)
Basic Facts about the United Nations, UN Publications (1995)
Blue and Beautiful Planet Earth Our Home, Ruth Rocha and Otavio Roth, UN Publications (1990)
Blue Helmets, The – A review of UN Peacekeeping, UN Publications (1995)
Charter of the United Nations and Statute of the International Court of Justice, UN Publications
Children and World Development, Roy Williams, UNICEF-UK and Richmond Publishing Ltd, UK (1987)
Descriptive Map of the United Nations, UN Publications
Everyone's United Nations, UN Publications
Human Development Report, UNDP (annual)
Human Rights: Questions and Answers, Department of Public Information, USA
Image and Reality, UN Publications
Introduction to the Model United Nations, UN Publications, 1992
Pepito's Speech at the United Nations, Margaret and John Travers-Moore, UN Publications, New York, USA (1985)
Pepito's Journey, John Travers-Moore, UN Publications, New York, USA (1987)
Pepito's World, John Travers-Moore, UN Publications, New York, USA (1988)
Rescue Mission: Planet Earth, Peace Child International, UN Publications, 1994
State of the Environment, UN Environment Programme, UN Publications
State of the World's Children, UNICEF (annual), UN Publications
Student Map of the United Nations, UN Publications
Teaching about Africa Recovery, UN Publications (1995)
Teaching about Literacy, UN Publications (1995)
Teaching about Palestine, UN Publications (1995)
Teaching about Peacekeeping, UN Publications (1995)
UN Chronicle, UN Publications
United Nations Convention on the Rights of the Child, UN Publications
UNESCO, Courier UNESCO (monthly journal)

United Nations in the 1990s: A Second Chance?, Max Jakobson, UN Publications, USA
Universal Declaration of Human Rights, Ruth Rocha and Otavio Roth, UN Publications (1988)
Women: Challenges to the Year 2000, UN Publications, USA
Universal Declaration of Human Rights: An Adaptation for Children, UN Publications, USA
World Bank Report, World Bank (annual)
World Food Report, Food and Agriculture Organization of the United Nations (annual)
World Health, World Health Organization (bi-monthly journal)
World Statistics in Brief, UN Publications

Videos

A Common Goal (UN activities through a soccer game, for children 8-12 years of age – Arabic, Chinese, English, French, Russian, Spanish)
About the UN (a series including videos on Peace-Keeping, Rights of the Child, Palestine, Africa Recovery, Environment and Development – English, Spanish, French)
Design for a Better World (an animated overview of the UN – English, French, Spanish, German, Japanese)
This is the United Nations (an overview – Arabic, English, French, Spanish, Japanese)
United Nations for a Better Future (an overview – Arabic, English, French, Spanish)
On Common Ground (a tour of the UN – English), UN Publications
Asimbonanga (on the struggle against apartheid – Arabic, English, French, Spanish)
Making their way (women's rights – Arabic, English, French, Spanish)
Ticket to Development (instances of development work – Arabic, English, French, Spanish)
Our Water, Our Lives (water and the environment – Arabic, English, French, Spanish)
Doctor in the Sky (animated short on the environment – Arabic, English, French, Spanish)
Nguyamyam (animated short for children on the limited resources of our planet – Arabic, English, French, Spanish)

United Nations databases

DUNDIS – Directory of United Nations Databases and Information Services
Palais des Nations, CH 1211 Geneva 10, Switzerland

UNESBIB
DIT, Information, Library and Archives Division, UNESCO, F-75352 Paris 07SP, France

DARE
UNESCO, Social and Human Resources Centre, 1 rue Mollis, F-75352 Paris 07SP, France

Online access through ECHO (European Commission Host Organization), L-1023 Luxembourg

The United Nations also has several databases on the Internet:
UN: gopher://gopher.un.org
WorldWideWeb:http://www.un.org
FAO: gopher://gopher.fao.org
IAEA: gopher.//nesirs01.iaea.or.at
ITU: gopher://info.itu.ch
UNDP: gopher://gopher.undp.org
UNEP: gopher://gopher.undp.org/ungophers/unep
UNESCO: gopher.//hpb.hwc.ca
UNICEF: gopher://gopher.hqfaus01.unicef.org
UN Volunteers: gopher://gopher.unv.ch
WHO: gopher://gopher.who.ch

The Right to Write – Letter-writing tips

Handy hints for writing letters requesting information

Many of the activities in this Kit require you, the learner, to research further into a topic. This will usually mean writing a letter. You should write whenever you feel the need for further information and not just in response to a particular activity.

This sheet is to help you write letters in the most effective way.

To whom

A United Nations department or Specialised Agency (see *Resource Point K*)
To your Member of Parliament or other representative
To a non-governmental organization
To an expert in a particular subject

Why?

To express your opinion
To obtain further information
To encourage a particular action

How?

- Address it properly – librarians or teachers can help you with names, correct titles and addresses
- Use your own words not those of someone else
- Be clear regarding the issue you are writing about
- Be brief
- Give reasons for your opinion
- Try to show understanding of other opinions
- Be constructive and suggest alternatives
- If you have expertise, share it
- Ask for a reply and to be kept informed if this is appropriate
- Ask questions but don't be too demanding
- Include a complete return address
- Type or use your own handwriting – so long as it can be read it doesn't matter which
- Use headed notepaper if possible but make sure you are authorised to use it if you do.
- Enclosing a stamped-addressed envelope

from *The Right to Write* by former US Congressman Morris K Udall

More handy hints

- Leave at least a month for a reply. Most non-governmental organizations and United Nations Information Centres have only limited resources – this is why your letter must be to the point and specific. It may take some time for them to reply.
- If you want information ask for it specifically – don't ask for 'everything you have on poverty'!
- If your letter starts with Dear Mr Smith or Mrs Jones, it should end with 'Yours sincerely'. If you are writing 'To whom it may concern' or 'Dear Sir or Madam' then you should sign off with 'Yours faithfully'.
- First paragraph – explain why you are writing and who you are.
- Second paragraph – state your case or request your information.
- Third paragraph – close on a positive note.